As Far As I Can See

A Memoir

Rosemary M. Colt

As Far As I Can See
A Memoir

By

Rosemary M. Colt

First Stillwater River Publications Edition

ISBN-10: 0-692-61135-5
ISBN-13: 978-069261135-7

1 2 3 4 5 6 7 8 9 10
Written by Rosemary M. Colt. Cover design by Dawn M. Porter.
Published by Stillwater River Publications, Glocester, RI, USA.

There are no words in the English language adequate to express my gratitude to my family, who make life possible, and to those friends who did so much to help both Len and me before and after his death. To Claudia and Graeme, Allen and Rhoda, Jane and to Hilary for his devotion to Len—thank you from the bottom of my heart.

Introduction

Early in the summer of 2011 my husband Len moved into Bridges, the dementia unit of Epoch, an assisted living facility in Providence, Rhode Island. In late August I left our home in Little Compton, a small seaside town southeast of Providence, and moved into Laurelmead, an independent living community next door to Epoch.

Soon after that I began to keep a journal. Len died a little over a year later, on September 26, 2012. A few months after his death I read over what I'd written, which was essentially the story of Len losing his grip on life; it didn't include everything that had gone before. Len and I had been together fifty-five years and so perhaps writing about our past would mitigate the sadness of our final months and calm my fears of the future.

As I thought back over leaving our home, Len's illness and his death, I sensed the outline of a story about two people from different backgrounds who married young and made it work. Over the years, Len and I changed each other in many ways. We grew up together and we kept on growing right to the end. Reflecting on our life together has been satisfying; it has also helped me to see a way forward without Len.

Providence, Rhode Island, 2015

1

I
Leaving Meadow Lane

I wake up early and lie in bed listening to the radio. It's August 25th, 2011, a Friday. After a while I get up, feed the cat and go around the house one more time, my footsteps echoing in the empty rooms. Going from one end of the long, narrow upstairs to the other, I walk past the closets under the eaves where the grandchildren used to play sardines, past the empty bookcases and the stacked boxes waiting to be carried off. On the way back downstairs I pause on the landing and look out at the barn. The first time Len and I saw it—and the house--was on a bright snowy day in the winter of 1963. Somewhere packed away, there's a picture of one-year-old-Nicholas taken then. Bundled up in a bright red snowsuit, he's sitting on a sled with a potty chair strapped on behind him.

Len's mother and father had just bought this house, which was part of a derelict dairy farm on thirty acres of land near a saltwater marsh. They were building a new house and turning the old house over to their children. As fate would have it, we would live in it for a year, beginning the following September. In the fall of 1963 Len was working in the sales department of Reed and Barton Silversmiths in Taunton, Massachusetts. We were living in a rented house in Raynham, a suburb of Taunton. Len's future was uncertain and we didn't want to be tied to a lease, so we moved to The Farm. There were few people our age around and I was cooped up with the three children, the oldest of whom, Ames, had just turned five. But it was a good house; our bedroom was on the first floor, along with the living room and the kitchen. Upstairs, there were four small bedrooms and a bathroom with a blue linoleum floor--the indoor plumbing was a mere five years old. It was a sunny house, with a view out across the meadows that made it seem larger.

The children loved playing in the dilapidated corncrib, a treasure trove of old cow bones and rusty nails. We made a sandbox in the stone foundation where a silo had been, although the feral cats liked it better than the children did. There was a barn for them to play in too, still redolent of the cows. In the fall, an ancient horse chestnut tree provided ammunition for sibling battles and for the first time in our married life, Len and I had a garden. We cleaned out mounds of trash that had been tossed into the fields and resurrected hedge roses and yuccas that bloomed in July, when their fragrance filled the air for a few brief weeks. Wild blackberry bushes curled over and around the crumbling stonewalls--I braved the briars to pick the fruit, but it was sour and full of Japanese beetles.

At the end of the following summer—the fall of 1964--we gathered up the three children and moved to St.

Paul, Minnesota. Len was now the junior man on the Reed and Barton sales force, and responsible for covering a large swath of the upper Midwest. He traveled mostly by car, driving hundreds of miles in good and bad weather alike. He was away from Monday to Friday, while I stayed home with the children in a new house in a strange community. Neither of us enjoyed the schedule and it took its toll. I'd never felt so alone and paradoxically, Len's absence made me more dependent on him. In time we made friends and life got better, but the routine never varied.

In 1969 Len was transferred to Pittsburgh, a smaller and more manageable territory. During our years away from Rhode Island, we returned to The Farm every summer—it was the one constant in our lives. When we moved back to Providence in 1971, it was primarily because Len had a new job and we wanted to be nearer to our families. It was also because we missed Little Compton and The Farm.

But this morning, the last morning, there's no time to dwell on the past. I go down to the kitchen and pause to look out at the meadows, which are dotted with bales of hay waiting to be collected. The view was important to us when we renovated the house in 1984 after deciding to move permanently to Little Compton. Naïve and enthusiastic in equal measure, we chose an architect based on our friendship and his glib tongue. Since he'd designed very few houses, and thus had little experience in vetting bids and hiring a contractor, building the house was an adventure. There were constant cost overruns, compromises and last minute crises. The day before we were to move in, a bulldozer working around the house fell into the antique septic tank. Despite the headaches, we ended up with a house we loved; we called it 10 Meadow Lane.

From dawn to dusk the house is filled with light, so even on a grey day it never seemed dark. Whenever I looked out at the fields my spirits rose, but now I feel only the sorrow of leaving them. As views go, it's not a dramatic one--the old stonewalls around the property limit it. Yet it gave me a sense of possibility and expansion, of everything that's the opposite of finality. It was comforting to watch the light change on the fields and the hedgerows, suggesting permanence when the transient seemed overwhelming. On the day of our daughter Paris's first wedding, I gave thanks for the beautiful day. Early on the morning of her husband's memorial service just a few years later, I looked out at the rain and prayed it would stop, which it did. On New Year's Eve 1999, the family chattering noisily in the living room, I stole away to watch the fields turn gold as the last sun of the century sank behind the woods to the West.

Those were the memorable moments, but what strikes me as I stand here for the last time is the sheer number of days passed, of meals eaten and nights slept in this house. We haven't lived any other place for so long. The memories contained within these walls encompass much of our life, including the gradual disintegration of Len's physical and mental health. Every time he was in the hospital, I came back to the comforting embrace of this house. Even when he wasn't physically present, it was filled with his spirit. He always returned, until the day a few weeks ago when he left for good. It was the worst day of my life and probably of his too, except he couldn't articulate his feelings. Playing out relentlessly, the day lives on in my mind.

***

The drive from Little Compton to Providence never seemed as short as this morning. The familiar landmarks go by swiftly--Windmill Hill, Gray's Ice Cream and the old granite mills in Fall River. We leave Rhode Island, pass through Massachusetts, come back into Rhode Island and suddenly we're crossing the bridge into the city. "Enter with a Happy Heart," says the wooden plaque at the entrance to Bridges when Len, Paris and I get there, a sentiment that seems at best ironic, at worst bizarre. I push the red button, the door clicks open and we enter, hardly with happy hearts. We've arrived at the place where Len will live out the rest of his days. We've tried to make him understand what's happening and why, but no one has had the heart to spell out the truth. We haven't told him he and I will never sleep in the same bed again or that he'll never wake to the fields he tended for fifty years. We haven't told him he's left his beloved home for the last time.

In the few weeks between deciding on Bridges and this morning, we've furnished his room. It's a pleasant space, with two long windows facing out on a courtyard. His father's maple bureau is against one wall, family photos arranged on it just as they were at home. A small leather box one of his sisters gave him some Christmases ago holds a few stray keys and a handful of foreign coins from our travels. The new bed is under the windows, a bulky green recliner, also new, fills one corner and the TV is hooked up. The most eye-catching thing in the room is the model of a clipper ship encased in glass, resting on top of a cedar bookcase. After his wife's early death, Len's maternal grandfather lived with Len's parents. He had his own apartment, furnished with pieces from a ship's cabin, of which the model is one. It's a reminder of the Sunday evenings when Len and his grandfather listened to their favorite radio shows together. He's retained that memory when so many others have slipped away.

We've also hung pictures. There's a large print of a clipper ship under full sail across from the bed, where Len can see it when he wakes up. Next to the bathroom door is a block print of farm animals he and I bought from a street peddler on a rainy afternoon in Beijing. Over the recliner hangs a watercolor of his parents' house in the Bahamas. For the wall by the door, I chose a photograph of the ranch in New Mexico where we used to go. The last time we were there was our final trip together. I've surrounded Len with reminders of our good times, which is why there's a watercolor of a villa in Italy he and I loved. It's not a great work of art—his mother bought it off the wall of a restaurant--but we were happy there. It hangs over the bed.

It doesn't take long to unpack and put away his clothes, all marked with his name and room number. We stow his toiletries—new toothpaste, new toothbrush, new shaving cream--in the bathroom cabinet and hang his bathrobe on the back of the door. I've done this before, so it's painfully familiar. Shortly after my mother's death in October 1986, I moved my father into a nursing home. He had dementia too, and although he could care for himself physically, he'd been dependent on my mother for everything else. Left alone in their apartment in Upstate New York, he was a lost soul. After a few months of trying to oversee him from a distance, I gave up and brought him to a nursing home in Rhode Island.

I wanted to be a good daughter, but with my mother gone my father shut down emotionally. In his worst moments he was angry with me and in his best, withdrawn. He couldn't accept his inability to live alone, nor could he accept my mother's death. He never understood why he had to leave the apartment that held all his memories of her. In time, he made a tentative peace with his situation as well as with me, but it was an uneasy truce.

The inability to make life tolerable for my father, along with the irrational resentment that he was no longer the father I'd adored, complicated our relationship. He was in the nursing home for just a year before he died. Len answered his angry phone calls, visited him, and kept telling me I'd done the right thing until I almost believed him. Now the past comes back to haunt me because I'm doing it again, except this time it's my husband and Len can't make me feel better.

I tell him I'll be moving to Providence shortly, but I haven't told him I won't be in the same room or even in the same building. Despite my efforts to prepare him for this, as the morning wears on he doesn't seem to realize what's happening. He's not angry, which makes it worse because if he doesn't protest, we can't know what he's thinking or counter the confusion he must feel. Towards noon, the director suggests that Paris and I leave--lunch, she claims, will distract him. She punches in the code to unlock the door and it shuts behind us with a decisive click and we get in the car and drive away. I try to imagine what's happening to Len and I want to turn back, but we make our way to the Mexican restaurant where Paris's son Gideon works. Busy with the noon rush, he gives us only a cursory nod. We go through the line and get food we don't want and try to eat it. The chatter is deafening and the music more so, but we're oblivious.

***

After lunch Paris drives me home and then heads back to Providence. I watch the car go out the driveway, down Meadow Lane and onto the road. Alone in the empty house, I finish the chores left undone in the morning. In the midst of folding the laundry I come across the last towel Len used. Then, sorting through a pile of his clothes destined for the thrift shop, I find a blue spiral notebook. Some months ago, Len had complained to his neurologist about his increasing memory problems. It was suggested he write down the names of family and close friends, so we stopped on the way home and bought the notebook. The handwriting is recognizably Len's, but it was already shaky. First on the list are close friends, followed by our neighbors on Meadow Lane and then our children and grandchildren, each name carefully spelled out.

I'm undone by the poignant evidence of his losing battle to hold onto memory and to his place in the world. Abandoning the laundry, I lie down on our bed and after a while the cat appears and curls up beside me, purring happily. Does she miss the warm body that belongs on the other side? My head's such a jumble I can't relax, let alone sleep. As far as I can see, which isn't very far, our world's been vaporized. Len's gone and our home of almost thirty years will be next.

Nor can I see my way clear to doing what needs to be done before moving day, just a few weeks away. The house has been sold after weeks of negotiation, but the buyers are difficult and the deal could fall apart. I don't want to leave this bedroom, where I always thought I would die looking out at the view. I don't want to move alone into an apartment. Despite the reassurances of the bank and my family, I don't know how we'll manage financially. I'm sick with anxiety, imagining Len alone in a strange place, unsure of where I am, unsure of where he is, lost. One friend assured me that putting Len in a facility would allow me to be his wife again rather than his nurse. She wanted to make me feel better and I understood what she meant, but I'm not convinced the two roles are mutually exclusive. Surely there are women strong enough to be both spouse and caregiver, but I'm apparently not one of them.

The cat wakes up and jumps off the bed. She's the last of a long line of felines. The first one came from the pound in El Paso, Texas, a bleak city on the Mexican border where we lived briefly when Len did his initial army training at Fort Bliss. It was the winter of 1961 and we'd been married for less than two years; I'd just turned 21 and was pregnant with our first child. Len went off every morning with the car, leaving me in our two and a half rooms wondering what on earth to do with myself. It was the moment when it dawned on me that Len's life was my life, like it or not.

Our apartment was the end unit of a one-story beige stucco complex that looked like a cheap motel. Frequent sand storms kept me trapped inside, although there wasn't anywhere to go. Bored silly, I felt life would be less lonely with a cat, so Len and I went to the pound one Saturday and came home with a little tabby, the first of many cats.

Over the years we also had two dogs, but cats were the constant. When Len's health began to fail in the winter of 2007, our resident feline was Maggie, an aging tabby with green eyes. When Len was in the hospital, I whispered my fears of the future to Maggie when I lay awake at night. Three years later, just as we made the decision to leave Little Compton, and just as Len began seriously to lose his mind, Maggie was diagnosed with a lung tumor. On a January afternoon a few weeks later, she was put to sleep in our bedroom.

Later, we took her body to be cremated and then stopped for supper on the way home. As we sat in gloomy silence, I realized what I'd tried so hard and so long to ignore, which was that Len had lost the ability to sustain a conversation. He wasn't able to express the sadness I knew he felt and from that day on, I associated Maggie's demise with his decline.

But we were not without a cat. The previous summer, I'd rescued a gray kitten that had sought refuge under a neighbor's porch. The last thing we needed was another cat, but it seemed as if fate delivered her to us. When Maggie died, Scusi had been with us for six months. She slept on our bed the first night Maggie was gone and every night thereafter. Len, an inveterate animal lover, talked constantly to her and if my back was turned, allowed her up on the table to clean his plate. I accused him of having tuna for lunch every day just because Scusi liked it. He seemed able to communicate with her in a way he couldn't with humans, at least not any more. Maybe it was because she had no expectations and made no demands. With Len gone, her presence is another painful reminder to me of his absence, of how empty the house is without him.

***

The days between Len's departure and mine pass quickly and at last it's my final morning in the house. There's no more time for daydreaming because the van is due in a few hours and I'm not ready. Turning away from the view of the meadows for the last time, I wash the breakfast dishes and put them in a box, empty and turn off the refrigerator and pack up what's left. Taking a last walk around the garden, I scatter Maggie's ashes in the same spot where Len buried the remains of earlier pets. Only he and I know where this is.

The van arrives, loads up and drives off to Providence. After checking the doors and windows to make sure they're closed and locked, I corral the cat and get her into the carrier. She and I leave the empty house and set out for Providence and a new life. The view from the kitchen window is lost to me and with it has gone my sense of continuity and safety. In front of me is a high wall blocking the view of what lies ahead as we begin all over again.

II

"Fragments Shored Against My Ruins"

Now that Len and I are settled in Providence, we've developed a routine. I try to get him outside every day to escape the airlessness of Bridges. The weather has been beautiful and I want to enjoy it before cooler days keep us inside. Len moves more haltingly on his walker now and this afternoon he stops more often than usual to rest on a bench. We stick to the path that goes around the green space in front of our two adjacent buildings, which stand at wide right angles to each other. I keep Len moving by reminding him that walking makes his legs stronger. Always a believer in exercise, always positive, he still talks of recovering, but from what he's not sure.

It's hard to find the right words to describe his frame of mind--perhaps intermittent acceptance. He seems to have settled fairly well into Bridges, especially since I've been at Laurelmead. It's been about three weeks now, so he's getting used to seeing me every day. He complains about where he is, sometimes vociferously, but I don't believe he's miserable and/or angry all the time—just sometimes. I suspect his lack of both short- and long-term memory makes home seem less vivid to him.

Our conversations focus on the moment, the blue sky and the breeze, the couple playing croquet. When we sit down to rest, I'm comforted by the familiar solidity of his body which, along with his smile, his gestures and his good humor, is unchanged. Sometimes it's enough for me-- sometimes it's not. Although the boy I married is visible in the man beside me, it's challenging to square our reality with memories of earlier days.

The boyfriend, the fiancé, the groom, the husband, the father of three and the grandfather of seven, they're all the same person and yet they're not. Nor am I the same woman, except that I am. But the core of what Len and I were remains. We've shared something special, he and I, and the memory of it will endure when he's gone. Now, especially now, I am driven to understand our life together before it ends. A character in a book I'm reading suggests that all we are in the end is a few unrelated images, a loose collection of memories. If so, I'm lucky to have so many.

***

Len and I go back to the fall of 1952, when I was fourteen and a 10th grader at Emma Willard, a girls' boarding school in Troy, New York. We lived in Ithaca, New York, and since my parents were not happy with the local high school, I was sent away for the last three years. In Ithaca, I'd made a friend named Terry, who spent her summers in a place I'd never heard of--Little Compton, Rhode Island. She regaled me with tales of its fabulous social life until it assumed an almost mythic significance for me. Her descriptions of beach parties, club dances and tennis and golf tournaments surrounded "Little Compton" with a golden aura. From time to time she even mentioned Len Colt, a denizen of this Brigadoon-like place.

When I wrote her in the fall of my first year at Emma Willard to report an upcoming tea dance with Salisbury, the boys' school Len attended, she told me to "sign up" for him. It was one of the arcane rituals of the times that if a girl knew someone at a visiting school, she could claim him ahead of time, thus limiting the chances of getting stuck. So I nervously penciling my name next to Len's on the list of attendees. When the day of the dance came, I put on the one pair of dress shoes we were allowed—black suede, low heels—and livened up my uniform blouse and skirt with a red belt with gold coins that jingled when I moved.

We assembled in the living room to meet the boys as they filed in from the bus. Len came down the stairs into the room, tall and gangly, in a navy school blazer. Terry had showed me a picture, so I recognized him. Did my heart stand still? Of course not. Was it the proverbial enchanted evening? No, I was just relieved he turned out to be as pleasant as he looked. Later, to tease me, he claimed he didn't want to get off the bus because he was afraid it would be a long night. We square-danced, an activity at which we were both inept, but he was funny and nice. When the evening ended I thought I'd like to see him again. I did, but not until the following summer, when I visited Terry in Little Compton and saw it for the first time.

The paradise I'd imagined was in reality a New England summer community like many others. Discreetly well-to-do families from Providence and Boston populated it in July and August, a few from as far away as New Jersey and New York. They lived in unostentatious comfort, or sometimes discomfort, in grey shingle houses built by their parents or grandparents. The golf club was simple, the beach rocky and the social life understated and family-oriented. It was a homogeneous population that viewed outsiders with a jaundiced eye. A vigilant real estate agent controlled rentals and sales to ensure that only the right people were allowed in.

Why did Little Compton seem unique to me? During my first year at Emma Willard, I'd been exposed to values that clashed with those absorbed from my parents. A scholarship student, the child of an academic household and a product of the public schools, I found myself among girls who'd gone to private day schools. Their fathers were mostly doctors and lawyers and businessmen. When I made friends with one of the few Jewish girls in our class, I encountered blatant anti-Semitism for the first time. I wasn't exactly naïve, but my sophistication—such as it was—was more intellectual than social. Because of my father's profession, I'd met a number of literary figures, especially following the publication of my father's recent biography of F. Scott Fitzgerald. I knew about homosexuality, I'd been taught that Jews and Blacks were my equals and I was used to the company of adults. On the other hand, I didn't know much about coming out parties, country clubs and second homes in Florida.

The teenagers of Little Compton—seemingly so self-assured—reminded me of the girls at Emma Willard. Part of me wanted what their world appeared to offer and I didn't think too hard about what it might lack. I sensed that a boy like Len might be the ticket of admission into that magic world, which unbeknownst to me, was to play such a large role in my life. But whatever I thought, Len had other ideas. I saw him only once during that first visit, at a dance at the golf club, which I attended with a date arranged by my friend. Costumed as a popular song—the theme of the evening--he and I were "How High is the Moon, How Deep is the Ocean." The boy draped seaweed around his white dinner jacket and I pinned a paper crescent moon on my head. Len was there, but he barely glanced in my direction.

I was not to be deterred; when fall came and Emma Willard was invited to Salisbury for a return tea dance, I signed up for Len again. I don't recall much about the evening, except that when it was over I thought I'd caught his attention. We had an especially good time together. I liked his sense of humor, his kindness, his blue eyes, and the fact that he was over six feet tall—I'm about 5'5"-- also appealed to me. Maybe it made me feel delicate, which I was not. On the bus ride back to school, I crossed my fingers. Miraculously, the next week I got a letter from Len, and then another. I answered, he responded and a regular correspondence ensued.

It's hard to exaggerate the status conferred by such visible proof of a boy friend at a prep school. It was ideal if the letters bore the logo of an Exeter or an Andover, but Salisbury was not to be sneezed at. Every day before lunch, we lined up in front of the stern-faced "mail lady," with her shoeboxes full of mail arranged in alphabetical order. If there was "the right" letter for one of us—from a boy, not a parent, a sibling or a friend--we tried not to gloat. Aside from its intrinsic value, it symbolized the possible acquisition of school scarves, stuffed animals, hats and other paraphernalia from the boy's school to wear or to display on one's bed.

I would learn in time that writing those letters was a true labor of love for Len, who was neither an easy writer nor a quick reader. But I appreciated them and saved them for years before they vanished in one of our many moves—probably thrown out by mistake. I was thrilled when one of them contained an invitation to a Valentine's Day dance at Salisbury, which I immediately accepted. On a chilly February morning, I took a bus to a village near the school, where Len met me. A hockey game at the outdoor rink, a frozen pond deep in the woods, followed lunch. Len was on the team, so I was left to stand in the cold for two hours, an ordeal made more tolerable by the sight of my name inked onto his hockey pants.

That night I wore my first grown-up formal dress, a black velvet halter-top with a sequin-dotted white tulle skirt. During a break, Len and I retired to the room designated as the senior smoker. I found myself sitting on his knees, and he kissed me. His lips felt slightly chapped, but soft and gentle. I'd just turned 16 and he was about to be 18, ready to graduate in June and start college in the fall. From that night on, we gradually became the focus of each other's life. Although it would be some time before I transferred my allegiance from my parents to Len, the transition began in that smoky room at Salisbury.

After that, I never felt entirely alone because I was with either my parents or Len. I'm not technically alone now, but these days Len leans on me. Just as the autumn sun warming us today will soon give way to winter cold, Len's health will worsen and I will lose him and I will be truly alone.

Len moves even more slowly when he's tired, so at the end of the afternoon when it's time to go back inside, I help him push the walker. I worry how we'll cope if he loses his ability to walk. Tonight, like most evenings, often with Paris's assistance, I sit with him at supper and help him get ready for bed. Once he's settled, I go back through the now-familiar corridors to the apartment.

Some nights I have dinner in the dining room, but other nights I follow Len's and my old routine and watch the news on TV with a glass of wine. Then I have my dinner on a tray with a book in front of me and go to bed and read until I fall asleep. I want to believe in the future, but the past keeps tugging at me because I can't see anything ahead but loss and sadness. Len's forgotten so much about our life that I feel compelled to remember for both of us. Our memories are an intrinsic part of our sense of our identity and without them, there's only the eternal present.

***

I met Len's family shortly after the dance at Salisbury, when Len invited me to come to Providence during spring vacation. The Colts lived in a large brick Georgian house near the Brown University campus, in a neighborhood not far from where we are now. We often drive by the house and I always remember when I first saw it. I'd taken the train from Ithaca to New York City and on up the Connecticut coast to Providence. When I arrived, Len and his parents were on their way home from a vacation in the Bahamas, so I was greeted by the youngest of his three sisters, Katharine, who came running down the stairs to welcome me. Later, she and I went to the airport to meet the family and my first sight of Len's mother and father was as they came down the steps from the plane, followed by him.

Despite his parents' warm reception, I was on edge throughout the visit. I didn't even like flushing the toilet, although I was housed in a third-floor guestroom safely out of range of anyone's hearing. It wasn't much like home. Our house in Ithaca was the first one my parents had owned. Before that, we'd lived in faculty housing, usually an apartment. My father, a child of the Great Depression, didn't believe in borrowing money. Instead, he used the cash he and my mother had accrued to buy our house in Ithaca without a mortgage, which strapped them for cash. It was a nice stone house with a big yard, but it was modest. My father's salary at Cornell was somewhere in the $5,000.00 range, decent for the times, but hardly lavish. Money was tight, especially after I went to Emma Willard. I'd never felt poor, but I hadn't felt rich either.

The Colts had a cook, a waitress at meals and a laundress who came in weekly. Nice as the family was, and they were very nice, I was afraid of using the wrong fork, wearing the wrong clothes or saying the wrong thing. It amuses me to wonder what they thought of me, if they thought anything at all, but they were unfailingly warm and generous and despite my nervousness, I liked them. Theirs seemed a warm and loving household. In time, I would learn that Len's parents always welcomed their children's friends and did all they could to make them feel comfortable--his three sisters were equally hospitable. I'd never minded being an only child, but their easy camaraderie was appealing.

One day, Len and I drove to Little Compton and walked around his parents' closed-up summer cottage. Situated right on the water, it was permeated with a damp salty odor from being shut up all winter. It was a pleasant smell, one I've associated with that day ever since. That night we went to a friend's house and watched "Carousel" on television, which in 1954 was still something of a novelty. Len told me he loved me.

Did I answer him? I can't remember, but I do remember that one of the songs from the movie was "If I Loved You," one line of which is "words wouldn't come in an easy way." In Virginia Woolf's novel *To the Lighthouse*, the main character, Mrs. Ramsay, is unwilling to tell her overbearing husband she loves him. I've always wondered whether this is her way of resisting the demands of his personality or because she can't articulate the complexity of her feelings. For me, silence always meant the latter. Len, the most straightforward, gentle man, the polar opposite of Mr. Ramsay, has always had a less questioning, a clearer and perhaps a truer sense of love than me. He never tried to intellectualize or analyze an emotion that defies analysis, while I never gave up trying.

***

The following summer, my father had a Fulbright grant to participate in an American studies program at Cambridge University, in England. In June my parents and I sailed from New York to Southampton on a Cunard liner, the stately Queen Elizabeth I. Len came to Ithaca just before we left and my mother told me years later it nearly broke her heart when she saw how hard I cried when he left. Admittedly, our five days at sea cheered me up. We were in third class, but even that lowest of levels had a touch of glamour. There was Baked Alaska for dessert every night and a stewardess in a white uniform drew salt-water baths for us. Some Emma Willard girls were in first class and I often made my way through the barriers to see them. One foggy morning, an aged Winston Churchill, wearing his signature a pea coat and holding a cigar, came out on the captain's bridge and raised his hand in the familiar V for Victory.

It was a wonderful summer, one that left me with a taste for travel. My mother and I lived with her aunt—my maternal grandmother was British--in a rambling brick house not far from the university, where my father was living. Auntie Olive was a tiny energetic woman whose husband had been killed in the Boer War and she'd managed all those years on her meager widow's pension. Edith, once her housekeeper, was now her companion. The former full-time gardener lived rent-free in a tiny cottage and tended the large vegetable and flower gardens in his spare time. The beds were lumpy, the house was cold and the only refrigeration was a stone larder.

Initially, my mother and I bicycled into town and bought fruit and cheese and biscuits to supplement the limited household diet—we were sick of broad beans from the garden. Our offerings were accepted, but so unwillingly-- Auntie Olive was proud--that we gave up and hid the extra rations in our bureau drawers. She was also a teetotaler. When my mother came back from sherry parties at the college with my father, she had to mask the smell of liquor on her breath.

Auntie Olive, however, was such a lively companion that none of the discomforts mattered. She told me endless stories about growing up in Newmarket and her adventures during two World Wars, when she'd been an air raid warden. One morning she was repairing the cover on an old throw pillow while we chatted. Peeling off layer after layer of fabric, she reminisced about which stage of her life each one represented, right back to the reign of Queen Victoria.

When my father wasn't teaching we explored the countryside with my mother's cousins and met more of the family. One of my great-uncles had been gassed at the first Battle of Ypres in World War I. He wheezed in an unsettling way and was in a wheelchair because he'd lost a leg. Everywhere we went we saw visible evidence of the damage wrought by World War II. In London, for instance, there was still much rebuilding to be done. Yet I loved England, from the tiny village churches to the awesome cathedrals and the great houses that were just beginning to be opened to the public.

I missed Len and wrote him almost daily. He kept those letters, and eventually they ended up in the box along with his to me. I wish I still had them, to keep company with the bits and pieces of our past that have made it here. Perhaps I'll needlepoint a pillow with a quotation from Eliot's "The Waste Land" that's part of the Fisher King's lament: "these fragments I have shored against my ruin."

III

An Evening in Bridges

I should make an effort to dwell less on the past and more on the present, but the latter isn't a lot of fun. Besides, much of what happens suggests to me something from the past. Perhaps I'm unconsciously trying to revive the Len I once knew by dwelling on our earlier days, but sometimes it's unavoidable. Last week, for instance, a notice appeared on the Bridges bulletin board announcing an upcoming "Family Night." Paris and I want the aides to know we're an attentive family, so we decided to go. It never occurred to me the evening would have anything to do with our early life together, but it did.

Even after nearly two months, Len has to be pushed to participate in the activities in Bridges. He claims they're a waste of time, but I suspect it's because it's hard for him to focus. A volunteer comes in to lead the residents in chair exercises and the aides play card and board games with them. Sometimes I think this is done as much for the sake of Bridge's advertised mission as for the residents. There seems a noticeable difference between the promises of the promotional literature and the reality of the place. Yet it's a good facility, better than most. Len is adjusting as well as can be expected and his essential good nature is still intact. I don't think he's enough in control of his feelings to put on an act, but I'll never know for sure because he can't articulate what it's like to be him.

When Paris and I get to Bridges on the appointed day, we have to cajole Len into going out into the courtyard, where tables are set up for the meal. He wants to know why supper isn't in the dining room as usual. Any change in the pattern of the day frets him, especially if it's late and he's tired. His sense of self depends on things happening when and where *he* thinks they should--like a child, he's soothed by routine. He finally gives in when we assure him there will be food. We sit by ourselves because we don't know the other families and no one asks us to join them. Once we're settled, an aide passes around orange Kool-Aid. Len always has white cranberry juice in the dining room that he half-persuades himself is wine, but there's no fooling him with the Kool-Aid.

But for me the Kool-Aid is the equivalent of Proust's madeleine—the taste of which revives the narrator's childhood so vividly. It reminds me of the "parties" we went to during our few months in El Paso. Except for the official teas on the base, which were boring, there were few social events. We had an occasional meal at the Officer's Club, but we were mostly on our own. The Kool-Aid materialized when we got together with Len's classmates and their wives at someone's apartment. We were always invited for 6:30, by which hour it was assumed we'd eaten dinner. The men were served beer and the ladies Kool-Aid, usually red. There

26

were about eight or ten of us newlyweds, mostly from the Midwest, and the majority of the women were pregnant.

One conversational topic of those evenings was how to clean the toilet seat when the men forgot to raise it. The difficulty of ironing their stiff cotton uniform shirts was also an issue. The women gathered on one side of the room, the men on the other, talking about sports or the rigors of army life, or so I imagined. But Len doesn't remember El Paso, so there's no point my bringing it up. The memory belongs to me alone now, but tonight it seems as vivid as the courtyard at Bridges.

After the Kool-Aid, we have chili in paper bowls, with cornbread on the side and a bean salad coated in a viscous dressing. The residents' prize for the most guests goes to Anna. A lively woman with dyed black hair, she once introduced herself to Paris as "staff," a dubious claim since she wore her panties over her slacks. Her table is crowded with relatives, all laughing and talking. One of the women plucks Anna's eyebrows and checks her chin for stray hairs. The other groups are quieter.

Some residents have no visitors or just one, a spouse or an adult child. No one joins us until after dessert, when one of the volunteers sits down at our table. She wants to know why Len never joins in the activities. Is she doing something wrong? We tell her he's probably frustrated by his inability to grasp what she's saying. I've watched her though, and her efforts escape the attention of most of the residents. She brings in copies of newspaper articles beyond their comprehension, and then lectures while they gaze at her blankly or nod off.

The awkwardness of the evening echoes my feelings about Bridges, but perhaps I resist believing Len's dementia is severe enough to merit his being there. I hated my father's nursing home because I thought there should be a better alternative, and I feel the same way about Bridges. Every time I come through the locked door, I think I should be caring for Len at home. I ask myself if he would have put me in an institution, all of which only delays my coming to terms with the reality.

As soon as it begins to get dark, earlier now because it's October, Paris and I take an increasingly restless Len back to his room and then go our separate ways. On balance, Family Night seems pointless to me. The residents were as unconscious of each other as ever and the families hardly mingled. If Len were Len, he would have jollied everyone along and joked about the awful food. Until his mind began to go and even afterwards, he was socially easier than me. He could always make conversation when he was tired or bored or when I fell silent, which was often. But I counted on him for a lot more than social banter. When I think back over the past four or five years, the gradual change in our relationship is apparent. As Len has become less able, it's fallen to me to make the major decisions, the most important of which has been this move. We were always equal partners, but the course of his life determined mine; now it's up to me alone.

IV

Childhood and Dependence

I understand my long reliance on Len. To begin with, he's been with me for over fifty years. Also, the nature of my childhood instinctively led me to seek out someone so reliable and loving. We met when we were 15 and 17 and married when we were 19 and 21, so there wasn't much time before him. But I was an only child, so life with my parents was more intense than if there'd been siblings. My mother and father's marriage was intellectually and emotionally close and I was always conscious they had a life apart from mine, but there were just the three of us and we were together a lot. It was a childhood that endowed me with a life-long feeling of self-worth and security and at the same time, a need for someone to lean on.

To begin with we moved a lot, which was unsettling for a shy only child. My father's first teaching job after graduating from Princeton with a Ph.D. in English was at Yale. He married my mother in 1935 and I was born in New

29

Haven in 1938. In 1941 he went to Wells College, in Aurora, New York, a tiny village on the shores of Lake Cayuga about forty minutes west of Ithaca. When World War II ended, he left Wells to head the English department at Carleton College, in Northfield, Minnesota. His final job was in the English Department at Cornell. Because of all our moves, I don't remember feeling completely at home anywhere until Len and I moved to Little Compton.

As a young child, I was subject to recurring bouts of pneumonia and thus didn't go to school regularly until the third grade. My mother tutored me at home, using a program developed for children of diplomats living abroad. In those early years, my father was to some extent the primary parent and certainly the most hands on. He rocked me when I couldn't sleep, taught me to ice skate, roller skate, hit a ball (not very well) and ride a bicycle. When I was sick, he read to me and played endless card games without seeming bored. He was always there, always patient, always loving and in return, I adored him.

My mother was more distant and more physically and emotional self-protective. She was the survivor of a chaotic childhood, with parents who gave and withheld love arbitrarily. Marriage to my father provided the security she needed, but I suspect she was still somewhat fragile. When I was about four, a second child, a boy, was born and died almost immediately. Both the pregnancy and the birth were difficult and my mother was in the hospital in Ithaca for nearly a month.

The baby died when he was about three weeks old, and it's a testament to my parents' protectiveness that I remember little about it except one visit to the hospital with my father. I think I saw the baby through the glass window of the nursery, but I'm not sure. He never seemed real to me and I don't remember feeling any loss. I don't even know why the baby died. My mother's physical weakness after his birth, let alone the trauma of his death, probably explains her self-protectiveness. I remember running towards her when my father and I came home from an outing around that time. She hugged herself closely and backed away, as if to ward off my pell-mell approach.

But if I sometimes longed for a mother who expressed her love more physically, at some level I understood her apprehension. I would comprehend it even better years later, when I recognized the same hesitancy in myself with regard to my own children. My mother was a naturally reticent person. I instinctively knew this didn't come from loving me less, but rather from her difficulty in expressing feeling, which to some extent I share. It didn't matter--I knew she loved me and I thought she was perfect. Often, I'd creep into my parents' bedroom and open her top bureau drawer, where she kept her few pieces of jewelry and her scarves, which smelled of Mary Chess cologne. I'd breathe in her scent for a few minutes, close the drawer and tiptoe out. In later years, we were to become very close.

Thus I was blessed with a steadfast, loving father who would do almost anything for his wife and child and a mother who gained strength from him and from our family life. It was a childhood that endowed me with a sense of the importance of security and love. My father's devotion to my mother, and hers to him, was a potent model.

***

One of the greatest gifts my parents gave me was the love of reading. Books and literary matters permeated our household. My father was an English teacher, a literary critic and for a while wrote both poetry and fiction; my mother was an aspiring novelist who spent hours typing away. There were often writers around and lots of talk about writing and academia with friends who lived primarily on the East Coast. For this reason alone, my parents—especially my mother—must have had mixed feelings about our move from Aurora to Minnesota in 1946. Born in British West Africa to a Swiss father and an English mother, she'd lived in England, Europe and Hawaii. Before coming to the United States for college, she went to boarding school in Switzerland, and didn't become an American citizen until she married. My mother seldom expressed nostalgia about her past, but the relative isolation of a small midwestern town must have been a shock.

Northfield boasted a population of about 5,000. The billboard on the edge of town promised, "Cows, Colleges and Contentment," which is what greeted us when we arrived from the East in the fall of 1946, having driven from Aurora in a drafty Buick convertible. I was eight years old. One of the town's claims to fame was the attempted robbery in 1876 of the First National Bank of Northfield by Jessie James and his gang. (What I could not have known was that my future husband's great-grandfather, General Adelbert Ames, went to Northfield in 1876 to establish what is still called the Ames Mill, where Malt-O-Meal cereal is made. Ames was present during the robbery, which fortunately for him was thwarted, as he had over $50,000 deposited in the bank, an enormous sum in those days.)

Set in the midst of flat farmland that stretched for miles in every direction, the town consisted of one main street, two movie theaters, a Carnegie Library and the grain mill. I could walk everywhere from our house. The Twin Cities of Minneapolis and St. Paul were an hour's drive north. Occasionally, my parents went there to catch up on foreign films or to visit friends on the faculty at the University of Minnesota. Otherwise, ours was a quiet household. My father went off to teach every morning while my mother worked on her writing. The irregular rat-a-tat of her Smith-Corona portable emanating from her makeshift desk in the pantry was the soundtrack of my childhood.

We lived in an apartment on the first floor of a modest house a few blocks from the campus. Most evenings, my mother read or wrote letters, while my father prepared for classes or graded papers. He was always ready to answer my questions about homework or to talk about what I was reading. On weekends, I often went with him to an athletic event at the college. He loved any and all sports and was a constant presence at games wherever he was teaching. Sometimes I tagged along with him to the deserted English department building and played teacher in one of the classrooms while he worked. Meanwhile, my mother kept on with her writing and did editing work on the side. Their social life consisted of going to the movies at one of Northfields' two theaters or gathering with with friends for a poker game around the dining room table during the winter or a kite-flying picnic in the spring or fall.

As one of the few children of an academic in the local school, a shy child and an Easterner as well, I was something of a social outcast. The other students were mostly the offspring of farmers and local merchants and my clothes were fatally different from theirs--wool knee socks and flannel jumpers with suspenders, ordered from the Best & Co. catalogue. The other girls wore heavy lisle stockings and cotton dresses, even in the cold weather. In the winter, I was the only one in bulky snow pants with suspenders. I was also shy after my years of homeschooling, and it's no wonder I lacked social confidence and was happiest being at home with my parents or doing things by myself.

There was something else that made me different; every June we farmed out the cat, packed up the car and headed east for the summer. My father had started work on a biography of F. Scott Fitzgerald, whose name was by then almost forgotten. His papers were at Princeton, so that's where we usually went. My father also taught at various summer schools in the East, but the book consumed most of his spare time. My mother worked along with him, transcribing letters and researching and typing the reference slips that would become the index. In fact, my father owed his book contract to her. Right after the war, she received a contract for a novel from Houghton Mifflin, in Boston. After a year or so of revising, they were still interested but wanted more work on the book, which she was unwilling to do. My father went with her to the meeting where this was discussed. As they left the office, she turned and asked the editor if he'd be interested in a biography of Fitzgerald because if so, her husband was thinking of writing one. He was interested, and a contract and some financial support followed.

If it sounds like the stereotypical story of the sacrificial wife sublimating her talents to her husband's, it wasn't. More than simply self-protective, my mother was unwilling to do anything she couldn't do perfectly. For instance, she gave up tennis because she knew she would never play at an advanced level. I believe she decided if she couldn't be a great writer, she wasn't going to settle for being merely a good one. Besides, she and my father enjoyed working together. The projects the two of them embarked on, beginning with the Fitzgerald book, gave her a sense of accomplishment without the danger of self-exposure.

The book changed our life. It, as well as Fitzgerald himself, became a fourth presence in the household. My parents often went off to interview Fitzgerald's friends and fellow writers and some of them came to visit. In the winter of 1948, which we spent in Princeton, Fitzgerald's daughter Scottie lent my father a number of family letters, scrapbooks and photo albums. My parents spent hours poring over them and if my hands were clean, I was allowed to look. The pictures of the three Fitzgeralds together, Scott, Zelda and Scottie, intrigued me. It was a family just like mine--a mother, a father and a daughter.

One day I listened to my parents reading aloud to each other some of Fitzgerald's letters to his daughter, written when he was in Hollywood and she was at Vassar. The evidence of his love for Scottie resonated with me because I recognized it from my own life. Scottie once told an interviewer she'd had a wonderful childhood. This might seem surprising in light of her family's troubled history, but I believed her.

One day years later, when my mother and I were cleaning out my father's office at Cornell, we found some of Scottie's letters to him in the back of a file cabinet. Flying home the next day, the letters in my suitcase, I saw Scottie's obituary in the newspaper, which seemed an eerie coincidence. Along with the article was a photo I remembered seeing of the Fitzgeralds arriving in New York by ship. Sporting a stylish cloche and standing between her parents, Scottie clutches a little suitcase and smiles for the camera.

In January 1951, our life became livelier when the biography, *The Far Side of Paradise*, was published. The literary world was ready for a Fitzgerald revival. Freed from the distractions of the Great Depression and World War II, his novels could be read as serious works. With the passage of time, Fitzgerald's life looked less pathetically messy and more tragically significant. By the modest standards of the day, my father became a media star. He was on the radio and in the newspapers and even in *Life* magazine, then a major publication. One memorable bit of publicity appeared in the *New York Herald Tribune*: "Young Professor Arthur Mizener," looking natty in a bow tie, holds up a cocktail shaker, as if about to enjoy a martini. The caption credits him with "unearthing the Cocktail Era" in American history. When we were in Minneapolis that winter, I saw a display of the book in a bookstore window. Glowing with pride, I felt lucky to have such a talented father.

A truer image of him appeared in the *Saturday Review*, in an article claiming that with "his wife and child, his profession and his consuming interest, he seems the authentic portrait of an integrated, happy man." I have a photograph of the happy man with his family taken in the summer of 1951, just after he left Carleton for Cornell. My mother and I sit side by side on a couch. An awkward thirteen-year-old with bangs, in blue jeans and a plaid shirt,

I'm clutching a black cat. My mother leans over to pat the cat and my father reaches a hand from his chair beside the couch to join hers. He has on shorts and a tee shirt, his standard summer garb, and his glasses and a manuscript are on his lap. It's how I remember the three of us.

***

My mother died at 73 in 1986, wasted by a long illness but in her right mind. My father died a year and a half later at 80, as much from heartbreak as from any physical cause, or so I think. He displayed little desire to go on after my mother's death, as by then she was the only person with whom he connected emotionally. At times I resented that my family and I were not enough to sustain life for him, but now I know better how he felt. He never mentioned my mother's name after her death. Only if I talked about her would he say it, and even then reluctantly. Nor was I ever sure he knew she was dead--sometimes it seemed as if he thought she'd just gone away for a while.

Although they never suggested I fell short of their expectations, my parents were a hard act to follow. Underlying feelings of inadequacy, buried for years, influenced some of my bad decisions, like leaving college after a year and a half. On the other hand, the example of their steadfast marriage motivated me to seek out something similar. In Len I found a man who offered the same unquestioning love my father has given to my mother and to me, as if the fates had hard wired me to look for him. The emotional inheritance of inadequacy on the one hand, and so much love on the other, embodies the truism that from those to whom much is given, much is asked.

Len's mother and father's marriage was also remarkably strong and neither he nor I ever considered divorce an option. Moreover, we grew to love each other's parents almost as much as we our own. They in turn were fond of each other and joined forces to celebrate with us in the good times and support us in the bad. Our mutual love for each other was one of the joys of our marriage. The four of them are buried side by side in Little Compton, in a plot they purchased together. I like to imagine them silently communicating with each other, watching over us from afar.

V

One Day at a Time

None of our parents ever faced a situation quite like ours, although my mother and I both cared for an ailing husband. Len's father died suddenly after an afternoon on the golf course, and my mother died in her own bed. Len's mother was a widow for many years and died in a nursing home alone, as did my father. Now here we are, Len slowly failing and me trying to get us through each day. As the fall progresses, I think we're both gradually adjusting, Len to Bridges and me to Laurelmead. Yet his questioning of where he is and what's happening continually challenges me. He doesn't retain anything for long and asks constantly where he'll go *when* he goes home, never *if.* When I ask him what he thinks of as home—looking for a clue to what he envisions--he pauses before answering. "Where you sleep," he says.

His uncertainty suggests he doesn't remember our house, even though sometimes he'll talk as if we're still living in Little Compton. Driving to a doctor's appointment, he'll worry that we're late because we didn't leave home early enough. I remind him we don't have to allow time to get to

Providence because we're already there. "Oh yes," he says, "I remember now." In a few minutes he worries again. He recognizes some of the houses we pass and asks who lives in them because, he says, he can't recall. Most of the people he's thinking of are either dead or living elsewhere. He doesn't remember either his family's house or where he and I lived. Sometimes when we're outside on the grounds here, he asks me to point out where I live in relation to him. As often as I explain it, he invariably asks again. His spatial sense seems gone and he can't orient himself either mentally or physically.

I often bring him over to the apartment to get him used to it and to get away from Bridges. He sits in front of the west-facing window, where it's warm, and we have tea and Scusi comes out of the bedroom and rubs against his legs, which pleases him. He looks around admiringly, noticing the painting of a Mediterranean seascape that used to hang in our Little Compton kitchen. He likes it, he says, adding that he doesn't quite recognize it.

None of the furniture seems familiar to him either, although nothing is new. He roams around the apartment as if looking for a comfortable place to sit. Sometimes I'll ask him if he remembers the inside of our house, trying to phrase the question so he won't feel inadequate if he doesn't, but I'm curious. His usual response is that he can't recall because it's too long ago. I ask him how long. Oh, months, he answers. This is a nice set-up, he says, as if he's never seen the apartment. He keeps saying we're lucky to be here, except "we" aren't really here. He never asks to stay.

His presence makes me uneasy because it reminds me of my father's visits to our house after he was in the nursing home. I'd closed up the Ithaca apartment and my parents' possessions were mixed in with ours. Like Len now, my father would look around with a puzzled expression, as if wondering why some things looked familiar. My tongue was tied by my guilt for having put him in a "facility."

I try to explain to Len what our things are doing in the apartment, assuring him it's his home too, even though it isn't. Whatever I say, he doesn't retain it. We're surrounded by what defined home for us--art, family furniture, photographs and souvenirs of trips. Nothing is where it belongs, but then neither are we. I should be grateful for Len's forgetfulness, but it makes me sad. Every time he comes, I have to tell him where to turn when we get off the elevator. He's always sorry when I tell him it's time to go back to Bridges, yet when he gets to his room he sinks onto the bed with a sigh of relief. He doesn't connect the two locations and my guess is he doesn't realize how close they are to each other.

Most of the time now, Len seems comfortable in Bridges, He greets me warmly when I appear, except when he's in an angry mood, which isn't often. It hurts when he lashes out, but I know the situation is the target, not me. On the whole, he treats the aides nicely. Sometimes he gets angry when they dress or shave him and he doesn't like them touching him— he'd rather take care of himself. Occasionally he'll glance over at a slumped body propped up in a wheelchair and tell me "that woman" ought to be in a nursing home. On the other hand, he seems to know he's in a facility, and asks frequently if he's well enough to go home yet. Sometimes he angrily says he *is* well enough and he wants to go home *today*, and orders me to start packing so we can leave immediately.

He's beginning to join in some of the activities. One day, a volunteer was quizzing the residents about their families.

Len remembered our children's names, although he stumbled over the grandchildren and the in-laws. He spoke of his mother and father with devotion and recalled quite a bit about them. The past is sometimes clearer to him than the present, although he confuses the chronology and mixes up the living and the dead.

Alas, the days are getting shorter and colder. Len repeatedly talks about going south, preferably to the Bahamas, which he remembers fondly. He's forgotten his parents' house was sold years ago, but when I remind him, he says it doesn't matter—any place will do as long as it's warm. He feels the cold more now, although I've always been the chilly one. He says he knows we can't manage a trip this year, but perhaps next year; I say that would be nice.

Len seems to know that most mornings I'll appear, though he thinks I come earlier than I do. Sometimes I find him in the living room with the other residents, which never happened during his first weeks there. There's no knowing what's really going on in his mind because his thinking is inconsistent. Sometimes when we're walking in the hallway, around and around to pass the time, he tries to explain what's wrong with him. I can't describe it, he'll say, but I know I'm not right. I struggle to explain in language he can grasp. There *is* something the matter, I say, your brain has taken a beating.

I keep trying to find the right words, words that don't condescend. In the end, I resort to soothing him, to assuring him he's not the "asshole" he claims to be. Sometimes he gets teary and worries that I'll get tired of "all this" and leave him. What's more, he says, he wouldn't blame me if I did. I tell him I'm not going to leave. He wouldn't have abandoned me, so why would I desert him? There's little I can do to stop him worrying when I'm not with him, but I'm not sure he does. It may be that when I'm not there, I'm simply not there, and with no reminder of his former life he lives in the present.

It's never seriously occurred to me to leave Len, least of all now. I'm here because it's my duty and because I want to be with him for the time we have left together. There are even some days when I see our situation as a gift. Len has taken better care of me than I of him, so perhaps now I can repay him some of what he's owed for the love and security he's given me in such large measure. In a funny way, I feel free to love him more completely, but free from what? Not from the bonds of marriage, because I've seldom found those restrictive.

Is it because Len is so helpless that loving him is like loving a baby, expecting nothing in return? No, he's still capable of expressing love, and does so frequently. Or maybe it's because it's just the two of us now. Our children and our grandchildren are essential to our sense of ourselves, but in fifty-plus years of marriage we've become a world that's populated by only the two of us. We still have that, now we're reduced to our essence, to the habit of loving each other. But— and it's a big but--we're not living together. Something has ended that began a long time ago, and a chapter has begun that we couldn't have anticipated.

VI

Waiting for Marriage: 1953-1957

In the years between meeting and getting married, we were either in school or at our respective homes. When I was a senior at Emma Willard, Len was a freshman at Middlebury College in Vermont, five hours away, even if I'd been allowed to have male visitors. We saw each other during vacations and a few times in the summers, and that was all. Our partings were sad and our reunions happy.

Absence seemed to make our hearts grow fonder and we were never together long enough for the glow to wear off. Nor did Little Compton lose its charm for me--my visits there were always too short. I always slept with his youngest sister, Katharine, whose room was on the second floor, up under the eaves of the roof. The house sat on the eastern shore of a large salt-water river that flows out to the sea and the room faced west. At night, I could hear the irregular bong of Old Bull, a bell buoy out in the middle of the river.

Looming over my senior year at Emma Willard was the dreaded college decision, but I couldn't focus on it. I was a diligent student and would have no trouble getting into a good place, but that didn't make the choice any easier. During the summer between junior and senior years, my parents and I visited Smith and Mount Holyoke, trudging around the deserted campuses in the August heat. I couldn't picture myself at either place, or anywhere else. There seemed no connection between what I felt about myself and the idea of college.

In the fall, we seniors were summoned to the guidance counselor's office one by one to discuss our choices. Essentially, we were told where the school wanted us to apply. I murmured something about Radcliffe, but when that was dismissed for reasons I can't recall, I finally settled on Vassar. My mother had gone there, which seemed as good a reason as any. She'd written for the literary magazine, acted in plays and been chosen for the famous Daisy Chain. If it worked for her, maybe it would work for me, so almost by default I applied and was accepted.

What my problem was is hard to say even now. I recognized the value of academics and wanted to learn, but there was a gap between knowing the right thing to do and being motivated to do it. I blame some of my malaise on the times; it was the 1950s, and though we were encouraged to think seriously about our futures, Emma Willard's influence on its students was limited. Few of us were imaginative enough to envision a career other than marriage and motherhood. Many of us would live to curse our shortsightedness, but not until much later.

Nor was Len responsible for my lack of direction; he always told me how lucky I was to have a choice of colleges, as his road hadn't been so easy. He wasn't an especially good student and academics were an effort for him. The truth is that I simply couldn't see beyond the present moment because the future seemed fuzzy. Nor did I have much self-confidence. Our son Nicholas once said of the same stage in his life, that he knew what he didn't want, but not what he wanted. Both of us came to regret our lack of foresight.

When September came, it fell to Len to deliver me to Vassar because my parents were in London for the academic year. My father had a Fulbright grant to research a new project. Also, he'd made a name for himself in England as an authority on American literature and was in demand as a speaker. In recent years, they'd made a second life in London. Neither he nor my mother was happy about leaving me for so long, but they felt that after three years at boarding school I was self-reliant. If I'd known it myself, I would have told them differently. Then there was Len, whom they knew well. Whatever they felt about the wisdom of our relationship, they trusted him to get me to college--maybe their faith in him even influenced their decision to go to England.

On the day they sailed, Len was with us at the docks in New York. The departure of a large ocean liner was always a festive event. My parents had invited some friends to see them off and we had a very jolly time until the sound of the ship's foghorn warned visitors to leave. At that moment, I faced the unhappy reality of nine long months without my mother and father. Life does funny things and it's possible I wouldn't have married Len if they'd stayed this side of the Atlantic that year because in their absence, he became my sole emotional support. A few days after they sailed, he drove me to Vassar, trunk, tennis racket and all. After helping me unpack, he went off to his junior year at Middlebury. I sat on the unmade bed in the bare single room, so lonely and unsure of myself that even going to the dining room for dinner loomed as an ordeal.

It was a shaky beginning to a long, strange year and Len was my anchor. I made friends easily enough, but I never felt part of college life. Instead, I lived for the few weekends when he could make the long trip from Middlebury to Poughkeepsie. At first he hitchhiked, but then his father took pity and bought him a secondhand car. I spent Thanksgiving in Providence with the Colts, the first holiday Len and I had been together. One set of relatives took me on for Christmas and another for spring vacation. By then, I was counting the days until June and the end of the school year.

I did not excel academically. After Emma Willard's rigorous preparation, most of my classes were repetitive. Two of my teachers were friends of my parents and I took advantage of their assumption that I was a good student. One of them had been a graduate student of my father's and I don't suppose he relished the idea of giving me an inferior grade. Consciously or unconsciously, they made allowances and so I got by, but little more. The only teacher who inspired real enthusiasm in me was a fiercely bright young woman who taught Art History, and who later made a name for herself as a critic.

How and when did Len and I come up with the idea of marriage? Odd as it sounds sound, the decision seemed to make itself. As my freshman year went by, we gradually assumed we would always be together. There were a few ups and downs in our relationship, but none of them serious. I knew marriage would limit my educational options, but whenever I thought about leaving Len, I couldn't imagine life without him—it was that simple. I can only assume he felt the same way because whenever I expressed doubts, he simply waited me out. He promised he was going to propose to me formally, but I don't remember that he ever did. Right after Christmas, we found ourselves talking generally about marriage, and then more specifically. So however it came about, the decision to marry took on a life of its own.

The possibility of marriage became more real when I spent a week in Middlebury during winter break. I stayed in a rooming house where the owner let us use the kitchen. Len and I marketed together and cooked up meals of hamburger and frozen peas that we ate on a card table in my room. Every night, Len went back to his fraternity house, making sure the vigilant landlady knew he'd gone. Others our age would have found this dull stuff, but we loved the domesticity and the feeling of safety. In the evenings, we drove around the village and imagined ourselves behind the lighted windows in a house of our own, together.

Len told his mother and father first. There was one phone booth on each floor of my dorm, which is where I sat one spring evening waiting for Len's call. Yes, he said, it was fine with them. He told me his father joked he hadn't known whether to send Len's tuition check to Vassar or Middlebury—our marriage would solve that problem. We agreed I would tell my parents when I saw them in June, as I couldn't imagine breaking the news to them during a transatlantic phone call. This was the 1950's after all, and I'd spoken to them only once in their absence, at Christmas.

At long last June came. Len drove me to New York and I sailed for England to join my parents. When the ship docked in Liverpool in the early morning, I went up on deck and hung over the rail until I saw them, two tiny figures waving at me from the pier below. My mother had on a bright green raincoat and my father a tweed cap that made me think of Mr. Toad in *Wind in the Willows*; I was so happy to see them.

We arrived at their London flat the next day. By then I'd worked up the courage to tell them Len and I wanted to get married the following summer and so at dinner I told them. I wish I could remember their response in more detail, but the upshot was my father's insistence on telegraphing the Colts to say how pleased he and my mother were. This still takes my breath away, but it was typical of my father. He and I went off to the telegraph office in the long evening light of early June. Many times since, I've imagined my mother doing the dishes back at the flat, wondering how it would all turn out.

I knew enough to be grateful for my parents' acceptance of the inevitable. It was not until much later, when we were confronted with our own children's marital decisions, that I truly appreciated what a leap of faith it was. It served them well, however, because their belief in us made it impossible to let them down; our parents' mutual assumption that our marriage was a good idea helped to ensure its endurance.

I also knew that abandoning my education to get married was foolish, but assumed I could go back to school at some later time. At the same time, I wasn't motivated by any particular career goals. I harbored a vague notion I might write, although I had nothing to write about. Marriage seemed like a safe harbor, as well as a way to avoid new situations. I couldn't imagine re-entering the dating game, which had always made me nervous. Most of all, it was a miracle to me that someone as nice as Len loved me, so how could I turn him down? I suspected, perhaps feared, that no one would ever love me as much as he did--and I may have been right.

More importantly, insofar as I knew what love was, I loved Len. He was safe, comfortable, kind, fun and by far the nicest boy/man I'd ever met other than my father. Additionally, there was the bonus of his wonderful family, who shared the values I'd grown up with. Hopelessly naïve as this was, I give myself credit for recognizing Len's fine qualities. Like my father, he was honest and reliable to a fault, as well as loyal and loving. It's silly, irrelevant really, still to be analyzing why Len and I married each other, but it amazes me that a marriage begun so innocently turned out to be so right.

***

Whatever doubts I had about marriage were dispelled by the whirlwind events of that summer. Len and his family came to Paris in June, where we met them. He and I picked out an engagement ring and celebrated with our families at a restaurant in the *Bois de Boulogne*. In July, the Colts hosted a dinner dance at a villa on the shores of Lake Como that belonged in part to my mother-in-law. A world-class party planner, Mrs. Colt gave a dinner, followed by dancing in the loggia—a sort of freestanding porch--high above the lake. Our friends who were in Europe that summer who came to Como for the party never forgot it.

After that, Len and I went to Rome with the Colts, where we saw Verdi's *Aida*, staged in the moonlight in the ruins of the Baths of Caracalla. It was the first opera we'd seen and we were smitten--our love for the art form began that night. We were to see *Aida* many times more, but it was never as wonderful as in Rome. Next, Len and I joined my mother and father in Pau, a small city in the French Pyrenees where my father was teaching American literature. The Colts, having overseen us in July, had turned us over to my parents for August.

Our train trip from Rome up the coast of Italy and into southwestern France took nearly 24 hours. We were in a compartment called a *couchette* that housed six passengers. Fastened to the walls above two facing banquettes were benches that came down at night for sleeping. We had nothing to eat all day but some ham rolls we bought at the stations where the train stopped. By evening, the roofs of our mouths were sore from the crusty bread. It was very hot, but if we opened the window clouds of dust and cinders blew in. Yet as we wound up the Italian Riviera and into France, the scenery was lovely and it was another new adventure.

We were alone until the late afternoon, when an Italian man joined us. Apparently he spoke no English, because he stared at us silently from the moment he stepped into the compartment. When night came, the three of us pulled down the "beds," stripped to our underwear and laid there in uncomfortable silence. The benches were hard and the Italian snored, so it was a relief to get off the train in the early morning hours at a town near Pau. As the train pulled into the station, I saw my faithful father standing on the deserted platform, his face illuminated by the glow of the single streetlight.

In Pau, we lived in a pension, a rambling nineteenth-century house called *La Rèsidence*, which was surrounded by a large, unkempt garden with tables scattered about under the trees. Referred to by the staff as *Monsieur le Fiancé*, Len was housed in the chauffeur's apartment over the garage, a safe distance from *Mademoiselle la* F*iancée's* room in the main house. Although he and I were not sleeping together—this was the 1950s, remember—he managed to make his way to my room at odd hours. My mother was an observant woman and I'm sure she knew this. Did she and my father wonder what we were up to? Did they worry? I'm sure they did, and crossed their fingers. Nowadays sex before marriage isn't an issue, but it was then, and for better or worse, it was a factor in many marriages. While sex definitely played a role in our eagerness to get married, it was matched by our desire just to be together.

Len and I rented a tiny Vespa scooter and rode around the countryside with me perched precariously on the back fender. On weekends, the four of us squeezed into my parents' Hillman Minx convertible, a miserable post-war English car, and explored further afield. One Sunday we went to Lourdes, the famous shrine. Packed in with a crowd of ill-smelling pilgrims, we toured the cave where Bernadette claimed to have seen the Virgin Mary. Another time, we followed the trail of Hemingway's novel 1926, *The Sun Also Rises*, an ambitious journey that took us down the coast and into Spain. We stopped in San Sebastian to swim and because we had no bathing suits, we rented them. I remember Len emerging nervously from the dressing room, self-conscious in a pair of scanty black knit trunks that would have been banned on an American beach. We spent a night in Pamplona and got flea bites from the bedding in Hemingway's hotel.

When the summer ended, Len and I knew we loved to travel. The four of us piled into the Hillman Minx one last time and drove north to Boulogne. It was a long journey for my mother and me because we shared the tiny back seat with a case of Spanish sherry. Despite the discomfort, what I remember most about the trip is how natural it seemed for the four of us to be together. At Boulogne, we crossed the Channel to Liverpool and boarded the ship to go home.

From New York, we took a train to Rhode Island for our engagement party, in the garden of the Colts' Little Compton house. It was a beautiful September evening, with the first chill of fall in the air. There were toasts and we threw our glasses into the well in the garden; it seemed perfect. The people Len and I were at the end of that magic summer are strangers to me now, but I look back on them with affection, and even a little envy.

VII
Getting Married

After the excitement of the summer, Len and I returned to college and waited for the wedding, set for August 10, 1957. I spent Thanksgiving in Providence and Len came to Ithaca for New Year's, but otherwise we saw each other on the occasional weekend. Meanwhile, plans for the wedding proceeded apace. With my sights set on the future, I couldn't focus on academics. I began to have trouble sleeping and fell seriously behind in my classes. By early spring, having worked myself into a state of nervous exhaustion, I went to see the college psychiatrist. A large, unsmiling woman in a starched white uniform, she lectured me about taking care of myself and ordered me to the infirmary for a few days.

Not surprisingly, this did little good and my mood only worsened. My distress had little to do with Len. More likely, it reflected the unarticulated sense that I was selling myself short by leaving college. Whatever the reason, staying at Vassar was anathema to me, so I called my parents and announced I wanted to come home. They tried valiantly to persuade me otherwise. When that failed, they enlisted the help of friends on the faculty, who fed me tea and cookies and good advice. It fell on deaf ears and at last my parents gave in. In late March, I packed up my belongings, said good-bye to my friends and boarded a train headed west. Gazing out the window as it wound through the countryside, I told myself I was doing the right thing.

When the train pulled into Syracuse, my parents were waiting for me on the platform. To their everlasting credit, neither of them said or did anything to make me feel guilty about leaving Vassar. Decades later, long after I'd finished college and graduate school, I tried to apologize to my mother for abandoning the education they'd worked hard to give me. When she replied that it really hadn't mattered, I was stunned—of course it mattered! On reflection, though, I understood what she meant. One's life is what it is and regrets are pointless, especially when that life has been good. Perhaps my mother was saying I'd been lucky to find Len, whatever the temporary cost.

Once settled in Ithaca, I got a job filing in an office at Cornell. At lunch time,I ate my sandwich in the cafeteria or if the weather was nice, outside on the lawn. I felt fortunate not to be one of students trudging by. Len came for a brief visit in June before going off to ROTC (Reserve Officers Training Corps) for six weeks, not to return until the day before the wedding. I spent the summer in a state of suspended animation, working and joining in my parents' social life. One evening they had a party for a poet friend who was giving a reading at the university. A beautiful young man with piercing blue eyes, he asked me what I wanted to be. As I struggled to think of an answer, he said of course, you want to be a writer, don't you? When I went to bed that night, I thought perhaps he was right, but it seemed unlikely. (Not long ago I saw him on TV, looking much older but still blue-eyed.)

In mid-July my mother and I addressed and mailed the wedding invitations. Soon the presents began to arrive, large boxes wrapped in silver paper and white ribbon, from which emerged silver vegetable dishes, silver cigarette lighters and ashtrays, linen placemats and monogrammed wastebaskets. Few of these things would have anything to do with our life for a long time, if ever, but they represented a safe, predictable future, which was what I wanted.

Len and his family arrived the day before the wedding. August 10th was a sticky, overcast day, but the weather cleared after an early morning shower or two. Two of my aunts put on a luncheon, and at 4:00 PM Len and I were married in the white stucco Episcopal Church in downtown Ithaca. The headmaster of Salisbury presided over the ceremony and a reception followed at one of the university clubs. There was wedding cake, champagne and tea sandwiches, the standard fare of the times.

Everyone looks happy in the wedding pictures. Our friends though, for whom marriage was a distant possibility, seemed bemused by it all. My memories are vivid, but scattered. I remember the heavy sweet smell of the stephanotis in my bouquet and the sweat on my father's brow as he and I waited to go down the aisle. My mother wore a bright green satin dress she never put on again and my mother-in-law was in cream-colored chiffon and a hat with a large upturned brim, neither of which she ever wore again either.

After the reception, Len and I drove to an inn in Cooperstown in our new Volkswagen convertible, which was white with red leather seats, a wedding present from Len's father. Arriving well after dark, we made a classic entry into the lobby, which was populated by elderly guests nodding over their newspapers. Exhausted as we were, what I remember most about the night is Len emerging from the bathroom in one of two pairs of Brooks Brothers monogrammed silk pajamas—one blue, one white—his mother had given him as a wedding present. The next morning we drove to New York and flew to Bermuda for two weeks.

***

In September, we packed up our belongings and moved into a small apartment on the second floor of the Catholic funeral home in Middlebury. The empty coffins were stored in the adjacent attic space, where I also kept our suitcases. Although the apartment was partially furnished, we had a few things of our own. I displayed our album of wedding pictures on the coffee table, along with the engraved silver tray that had been a gift from Len's ushers.

Len went to class every day and I got a job filing in a dean's office at the college. After a few months, I switched to a sales job in the local ski shop, where my co-worker was a pretty German girl about my age. Christina's husband Jürgen was a new hire in the German department. She and I became good friends and we passed the time between sales comparing notes on cooking and housework, both of which were something of a mystery to us. Although I was bored silly, I felt sure life would improve once the year was over.

Eventually Len and I met Jürgen and the four of us went to the movies together occasionally and took walks when the weather improved. One day Jürgen, who was ten years older, mentioned that as a teenager, he'd been conscripted into Hitler's army in the last days of the war. After nearly being killed, he was captured and imprisoned by the Americans, which saved his life. Len and I were stunned when we heard his story. He and Christina, both gentle people, had experienced loss, hunger and a good deal else beyond our imaginings.

How naïve we must have seemed to them—they'd lived a lifetime, and we'd hardly begun. Compared to what they'd endured, Len and I were babes in the woods. The sense of unreality I'd felt since our engagement intensified. We seemed to be playing at marriage. Still dependent on the generosity of our parents, we had yet to define ourselves as a separate unit. I told myself this would come in due time, but I wondered when—perhaps when Len went into the Army, which wouldn't be until January. There was nothing to do but wait. Meanwhile, Len graduated from Middlebury and we went back to Providence for the summer. I couldn't know that in the fall, in faraway London, our life would begin in earnest.

VIII

Religion, Politics and Conformity

Meanwhile, we were gradually getting used to each other. There were differences between Len and me that could have handicapped our chances for a happy marriage if we'd let them. They were evident, for instance, in our religious and political views. We were still young enough to be under the influence of our upbringings, which had been different. Before we married, neither of us gave this much thought, which alone suggests our lack of maturity. I knew I cared more about issues than Len, politics for instance, but this didn't seem a barrier to marriage—little did I know what a potential pitfall it was. Occasionally I was irritated when Len seemed unaware of what I considered glaring flaws in, for instance, an institution, but I already knew he was a more tolerant person, usually willing to let the world be what it was.

Len had been raised a serious Episcopalian, so it was natural for him to go to church; in Little Compton, for

59

instance, he was a regular at the Congregational church. Thus I'm not surprised when I arrive in Bridges one Sunday morning and find him partaking in a service in the living room. A Catholic priest, fully robed, stands in front of a makeshift altar, complete with cross, prayer book and communion chalice. I sit down next to Len, who seems to be enjoying himself. When the service ends, he assures me the priest is a "nice man." This, along with "good man," is his strongest form of praise. In the past, I've usually responded tartly by asking him how he knows this, but not anymore.

Every Sunday from then on, I make sure he goes to the service since it seems to mean something to him. It also provides a focus for the slowest day of the week. As the November afternoons grow shorter and we're inside more, keeping Len entertained is difficult, especially on weekends, when planned activities are few and far between. T.S. Eliot's "The Waste Land" claims April is the cruelest month, but I say it's November, when the dark descends earlier every day and it's often too cold to be outside for more than fifteen minutes.

At the service, Len bows his head when the priest prays and mumbles the words of the Lord's Prayer along with him. He accepts the communion wafer when it's offered, although he has to be shown how to hold his hands to receive it. I can't tell if he's befuddled or soothed, but he seems to recognize the spiritual element of the occasion. One Sunday morning, I hear him tell his neighbor that as a boy he was an acolyte. I suspect he's advertising his religious credentials as well as affirming that he once had a life. I've thought about taking him to the nearby Episcopal Church, which is where he was an acolyte, but the logistics of getting him there defeat me.

Then I see an announcement for an Episcopal Eucharist, to be held in the chapel at Laurelmead. I didn't know there was a chapel, but then I remember the stained glass windows in the sales manager's office. They struck me as unusual, but perhaps the room had been a chapel and still served as such when needed. I inquire and learn that yes, this is so. Thus one Sunday morning we make our way to the "chapel," where we interrupt an elderly gentleman who's changing into a cassock. He peers intently at Len, introduces himself, and tells me the two of them served as acolytes together which seems a good omen.

The room has been temporarily reconfigured as a chapel, with a dozen or so chairs in rows. Soon a handful of residents trickle in, and they seem pleased to see newcomers. The priest begins the service with a homily that threatens to go on forever. Knowing communion is yet to come, I worry that Len will get restless or sneeze loudly or need the bathroom and I'm relieved when we make it through the hour. Len pays little attention to the service and I can't see that it means much to him. The congregation asks us to join them for brunch, but I decline, claiming it would be too tiring for Len, which is true. Despite their warm welcome, I know we won't return. Len seems happy at the Catholic service in Bridges and if there is a God, surely He or She is present in both places.

***

Back in his room after the service, Len sleeping soundly, I think about our different views towards religion and ritual. Neither of my parents was religious or even spiritually minded. I doubt if my mother ever willingly saw the inside of a church after her baptism as an infant. She avoided any ceremony that smacked of religion, especially funerals, for which she had a special antipathy I never fully understood except for the obvious. My father respected the proprieties and could look solemn when required, but his only god was literature.

I was first exposed to church at my christening—I was about five--at the Presbyterian Church in Aurora, which I believe was done solely to placate my paternal grandmother. She was not an especially religious woman, but she probably believed in the importance of ritual, which to some extent my father did too. My godparents presented me with four coin silver teaspoons, hardly the gift to thrill a small child. This was the extent of my religious life until we moved to Northfield, where elementary school students were dismissed from class every Wednesday morning and transported to the church of their choice for religious instruction. After some discussion, my parents, who didn't belong to any denomination, decided I should go to the Episcopal Church. Since the other options were the Lutheran and the Catholic, this must have seemed a natural.

We Episcopalians were a small group. The so-called classes were held in the basement of a little white frame church, which was badly in need of a paint job. A female parishioner conducted the class. What I remember most about those mornings is the janitor exposing himself to the girls in the furnace room. We must have been more fascinated than shocked because we never reported him either to the authorities or to our parents. I remember too the acrid smell of the coal that heated the church.

Later, I was confirmed because that's what everyone did. My parents dutifully attended Christmas pageants, Easter concerts and the like, but I knew their hearts weren't in it. I'd like to think I was an independent thinker, but I wasn't. "Fitting in" was important to me and I was often torn between my parents' discreet non-conformism and the desire to blend into the social milieu of a small midwestern town. Deep down, I thought my parents were right and I suspected my values were inherently the same as theirs. I lacked, however, the self-confidence to act on my instincts. I knew church school was boring, and confirmation a silly idea, but I went along. Years later, as I've said, I felt a similar but more serious conflict between the values I had been taught and those of the other girls at Emma Willard

It was hard to reconcile what I believed with an adolescent's longing to fit in, and I envied my parents' seeming ability to pass muster in a variety of social situations when necessary. My father had grown up in Erie, Pennsylvania, a small city with a social life resembling the country club world of John O'Hara's novels. My mother's background was more exotic, and her Vassar degree added a dash of respectability. But my parents' values were those of the academic world and their politics were decidedly left wing.

In my teens, I was torn between my admiration for them and a strong desire to belong socially. The need for protective coverage was, quite honestly, part of Len's appeal. He and his family were socially acceptable and they represented a world to which I thought I wanted to belong.

The irony is that Len himself was a true democrat who never considered the finer points of social discrimination. He was one of the most accepting and inclusive people I've ever known.

***

When it came to that other touchiest of subjects, politics, Len and I started out in opposite camps. He was raised in a moderate but definitely Republican household. While his mother was active in Republican politics in Rhode Island, my parents would have walked the plank rather than vote for a Republican, especially my mother. In 1948—Truman v. Dewey--she cast her ballot for the Socialist candidate, Norman Thomas, which created a sensation when announced to my third-grade classroom. It's difficult to imagine, but the teacher had asked us to tell the class whom our parents were voting for. I suspect that except for me, it was a landslide for Thomas Dewey.

My father voted for Truman that year. I woke up late on election night—or early the next morning--and found him in the living room with his ear bent close to the radio, silently cheering as Truman pulled ahead of Dewey. His earlier political views had been less in the mainstream and he always believed that his contract at Yale—his first job after graduate school—was terminated because he was too liberal. During my parents' first year together in New Haven, the local Communist Party approached my mother. She decided she wasn't interested, and was infuriated when she learned they'd been after my father and not her. He wouldn't have gone that far, but he held strong views even for the times.

When Adlai Stevenson ran for president in the fall of 1952, my parents threw themselves into his campaign with gusto and when he lost, my mother retired to her bed for two days. In 1962, John Kennedy was my Adlai Stevenson. It was the first election in which I was old enough to vote and I saw it as my chance to save the world. When Len voted for Eisenhower in 1958 I wasn't pleased, but since I couldn't vote I wasn't as focused on the election. Also, even I recognized that Adlai Stevenson's second bid was a lost cause.

On the contrary, in 1962 I was sure that JFK would be a great president who would make America a better country. Len's innocent announcement that he might vote for Nixon thus provoked a series of door-slamming arguments, especially after the debates, which I felt were conclusive evidence that Nixon was a thug. There were a few times that fall, however, when calm prevailed. Both candidates came to towns near us because New Jersey, where we were living, was a key state. We joined the cheering crowds and held up our toddler son to see the future president of the United States, whoever he might be.

On Election Day, I walked to the polling place pushing Ames in his stroller, only to be told I couldn't take him into the voting booth. Holding the stroller at arm's length but on the other side of the curtain, I leaned forward and pulled the lever. Len must have voted earlier in the day because he wasn't with me, which was just as well, as he did vote for Nixon. I spent election night dozing on the couch in front of the TV until the news came in the early morning that Kennedy appeared to have won. Len was a much better loser than I would have been. He lived not only to regret his vote for Nixon, but also to admit it—which I wouldn't have. He never voted for another Republican in a national election.

Returning to the topic of religion, Len was, as I've said, raised an Episcopalian. Moreover, Salisbury was an Episcopal school, overseen by a stern priest-headmaster. On the weekends I was there, Sunday morning chapel was required even for female guests and I could see that Len took it seriously. In retrospect, I think Len's fondness for church reflected his belief in the importance of community and for lack of a better term, fellowship. He didn't approach life on an intellectual level and I don't think he worried much about theological issues.

For the most part, Len saw the world as a benign place that might well include a beneficent God. I envied him his certainties and there seemed no reason to argue against them. For a brief time before we were married, Len talked about getting a theological degree and becoming a school chaplain. We even talked to one of the Cornell chaplains about this. The idea that we even considered such a thing— me as a minister's wife—boggles the mind. Len might have made an excellent chaplain, but getting through seminary would have been another matter.

***

One Sunday in November, after the service at Bridges, I take Len to Little Compton for the first time since he left in July. I don't think about that when we set off, only that we need a change of scene. It's not until we drive into the village that I wonder if it's a good idea, and then it's too late. We have lunch in the restaurant across from the United Congregational Church, Len's church. He chose it over the

Episcopal Church because he admired the minister. He also thought it was the more community-oriented of the two, which mattered to him. Peering out at the church, Len asks me if "that" was where he went. I say yes, almost every Sunday. I remind him that when he couldn't drive any more, his friend Hilary took him. I worry that the sight of the church might be a disturbing reminder of the past for him. As we leave the restaurant, he asks if he'll be going there again. Maybe, I say, and we get into the car.

I'd planned to drive by our house after lunch, but at the last minute I change my mind. I'm never sure how much Len remembers, and I'm afraid the sight of the house will upset him or that he'll ask questions I can't answer about why we're not living there. Instead, we drive down to Sakonnet Point and park and look out at the ocean. Then we drive back to Providence in the dying light of the November afternoon. It's the last time Len will see either the ocean or Little Compton.

IX
The Holidays

November is coming to an end and the dreaded holidays loom. After we moved to Little Compton, we usually had Thanksgiving at 10 Meadow Lane; it was "our" holiday. Before that, we went to Len's aunt's house, which was also in Little Compton. She'd modeled it on a seventeenth-century farmhouse and the dining room had a large open fireplace with a Colonial rifle mounted over it. It felt right for the occasion, as did the landscape of Little Compton. Our land lay between the woods where Native Americans lived in the winter and their summer campground, which was nearer the ocean. I liked to think of them going back and forth over the fields in the autumn, storing up food for the winter.

At Thanksgiving time a year ago, I was pretty sure that Len and I had to leave Little Compton. Seated at the head of the table, Len's grandparents' table, with its three leaves, all the family around me, I hated thinking it might be our last holiday there. The next day I told the children my decision and soon afterwards, on a cold, grey afternoon, Len and I visited Laurelmead for the first time. It's hard to believe it was just twelve months ago.

This year, 10 Meadow Lane no more, we go to Paris and Jim's for dinner. Our sons Nicholas and Ames and their families are with us too. We make a fuss over Len and he has a wonderful time, laughing and joking with his children and his grandchildren. Perhaps being with family allows the reality of his life to fade for a few hours. When I take him back to his room, he settles in happily. Thanksgiving wasn't the same without Little Compton, but it wasn't so bad either.

Christmas comes next, with all its emotional baggage--Santa's bulging sack of memories, each a reminder of what used to be, or the way we like to think it was. Truthfully, neither Len nor I ever seriously missed the hectic Christmases when the children were little. There were some wonderfully comic and happy moments to remember, but it was always exhausting. It's hard to imagine, for instance, how we survived in 1962. Nicholas had been born in early December, Ames was three and a half and Paris only a year and a half. At the end of that Christmas day, we collapsed next to the tree, stunned with fatigue.

Now we have to start from scratch to make new rituals. The plan is for Len to come to the apartment for Christmas Eve dinner along with some family. I've hardly cooked since moving here, but I spend the morning in the kitchen. I listen to the Twelve Lessons and Carols from King's Chapel in Cambridge, England, which is broadcast every year. I remember Auntie Olive telling me she always went, lining up early to get a good seat.

Len and I are joined by Ames and his son Alex and by my cousins, Ann and Dick, who arrive wearing Santa

Claus hats and bringing champagne. We all try to be festive and in a way it works. Len manages well, but he gets tired as soon as dinner is over. Everyone leaves and I take him back to his room and get him ready for bed, assuring him I'll be in early in the morning. I think he's already forgotten tomorrow is Christmas.

It's quiet when I return to the apartment, with the special stillness of Christmas Eve. Standing out on the balcony, I gaze into the dark, silent world. There are few stars to be seen and no trace of the moon. Len's and my future seems as invisible to me as the horizon. Later, waiting for sleep to come, I think about what it was like being a child on Christmas Eve, and the unbearable suspense of waiting. Len and I used to lie awake on Christmas Eve and talk about our childhood memories. I wonder what he's thinking about now, alone in his room, or if he's already fallen asleep.

One of my first Christmas memories is of my father carrying me down the stairs on Christmas morning. Though I can't see her, I sense my mother's presence. There is color and light all around me and the scent of pine fills the air. Then the black closes in again and I'm left wondering if this really happened, or if I've only been told about it—but it's so vivid I think it must have been real. A second memory is clearer; I'm five or six now and it's late on Christmas Eve. Too excited to sleep, I wander out into the hall and peer down over the banister. To my astonishment, I see my father setting out presents under the tree, which he always put up and decorated after I was in bed.

I'd assumed it was Santa who did everything, but here was evidence to the contrary. I watch as my father arranges some green and black books on a small bookcase.

The next morning, I'll discover this is his childhood edition of the *Book of Knowledge*, complete with its own maple shelf. I loved those books and spent hours reading them. I especially enjoyed the lives of the saints--my favorite was Saint Joan, depicted in full armor with her sword in hand.

What I saw over the bannister that night proved Santa didn't exist, but this didn't make me sad. After all, there were still presents. The tree was still hung with angel hair that cut your fingers if you weren't careful, and glittering ropes of tinsel and brightly colored balls. The angel with her white dress and glass halo still perched on top, where she belonged. (The same angel, a little the worse for wear, with a new skirt made out of one of Len's handkerchiefs, would grace our children's trees for many years.)

I doubt Len remembers it now, but he used to love recalling his father dressing up as Santa when he was little. His mother would wake him and his younger sister and allow them to peck down into the living room. His Christmas rituals were more elaborate than mine ever were. The Colts dressed formally for an elegant dinner on Christmas Eve. Breakfast was fried chicken with cream gravy, followed at noon by another festive meal. I, on the other hand, spent the day reading new books and playing new games, quite convinced that no one could have a better Christmas. Our memories were different, but equally happy.

I go to bed, wondering what new memories we'll be making now. Christmas morning is cold and grey, with a little light snow drifting down. I set out for a long walk that takes me by the house where we lived in the 1970s and early 1980s. Then I go past our first apartment, where Paris and Nicholas were born just eighteen months apart—the site of that hectic Christmas. The woman I was then, an exhausted mother of three, could not have imagined today. I pause in front of the apartment's living room windows, which face the street, but there's no sign of life and no visible Christmas tree.

The walk leaves me pleasantly tired. Stopping in to see Len, I remind him we'll be going to Paris's later and I lay out his blue blazer, his grey flannels and the Santa Claus tie he always wears on Christmas. When I go back in the late afternoon, he's sitting in the recliner, dressed and waiting. Bridges is very quiet. The city streets are quiet too, but Paris's neighborhood is ablaze with lights. Inside the house, the tree sparkles and there are presents piled high underneath it. After dinner we sit around the fire and open our gifts, the troubles of the moment fade and life seems good. Perhaps if I close my eyes for a few minutes, when I open them we'll be back in 10 Meadow Lane and the last few months will be a bad dream.

***

Thus we survive Christmas, but New Year's remains. Even at its best, this was never our favorite holiday. This year, Len will fall asleep at his usual 7:30, but I have to think about myself. A party is scheduled at Laurelmead, where holidays are routinely celebrated with special meals and entertainment. I can't imagine myself participating, not yet, but neither do I want to sit alone in the apartment. For lack of an alternative, I accept an invitation to a party in Little Compton. Thus, late on the afternoon of the 31st, I get in the car and drive there.

Ten minutes after arriving at my hosts' house, I know it's a mistake to have come. Rightly proud of the elegance of their house and its contents, they show me their latest acquisition, a massive Elizabethan oak bed with an elaborate tapestry canopy. I hope I won't have to sleep in it. I resent how serenely their life has progressed, whereas mine has gone so disastrously wrong. It's unfair of me—they're old friends trying to do something nice, but fair or not, I spend the evening muffled in a cloud of self-pity.

Dinner seems to go on forever. There are long pauses between courses while the host reads Internet jokes out loud. I know from experience to expect this and it shouldn't bother me, but it does. Everything bothers me. No one mentions Len's name, not once. Maybe they think it will make me sad, but instead it seems as if he's already dead. There's an explanation for this—people tend to feel awkward confronted with a situation like ours. They can't think what to say, so they say nothing. I've been in the same position myself and I should let it go, but I don't. I sense one couple I don't know well trying to figure it out. Where IS her husband? Dead? Ill? I recognize that my sullenness has to do with me and not with the evening, which is in reality very pleasant. I've no one to blame but myself, but I can't snap out of it.

In the morning I go back to Providence right after breakfast, lecturing myself for having behaved like a spoiled child the night before. When I get back to Laurelmead, I take a walk, shed a few tears of self-pity and fatigue and pull myself together. It's a gorgeous day, unusually warm for January. The exercise revives me and life seems less bleak. I gather up Len and we meet our friends Rhoda and Allen for lunch at a Chinese restaurant. Len enjoys the outing and manages the excitement well, although the chopsticks defeat him just as they always have.

The four of us laugh a lot and the unhappiness of the night before fades. Maybe I can manage this life after all, and maybe the coming year won't be so bad. I'm relieved the holidays have ended and that we've made it through. It's difficult to imagine what another New Year's will bring, but it's best not to know. I've spent most of my life anticipating the worst, a turn of mind Len always discouraged. He believed in assuming all would turn out for the best. My theory was that if something turned out better than expected, it would be a pleasant surprise, which is on the whole how the holidays have been.

X

Tears, Poetry and Music

It's 2012, the start of the first full year of our new life. I thought the end of the holidays would be a relief, but it's not. From New Year's on, stupid things have made me cry. Sometimes it's the music in exercise class—some song Len loved--or the sight of his favorite foods in the supermarket, a bad dream, or the shock of waking up alone in the morning. And it's January, bloody January, always a time for sobering thoughts. Troubled by all the tears, I consult the nurse here, who assures me the sadness I feel is normal "under the circumstances," a wonderfully vague phrase covering a multitude of the problems plaguing her aging constituency. But I feel that such constant weeping is excessive, and there's also something comic it. But as Adlai Stevenson said when he lost his first run for the presidency, it hurts too much to laugh.

I turn to literature for help, starting with Tennyson's poem "Tears, Idle Tears" because it seems appropriate. Perhaps it will provide perspective, coherence, as well as the comfort of knowing that others wiser than me have experienced despair and fear of the unknown, the pervasive sadness of Len's dementia and the possibility of his death. I find the poem in my battered copy of *The Norton Anthology of English Literature*, the bulky two-volume-series that was the primary text for students and teachers of English literature from the 1960s on.

The Tennyson section is in the second volume, the one with the murky Whistler painting on the dust jacket. Its flimsy pages are thick with my notes from over the years. Alfred, Lord Tennyson falls between Elizabeth Barrett Browning and Edward Fitzgerald. It was with the help of the *Norton* that I first felt the full power of poetry. The University of Minnesota—we were living in St. Paul--had just initiated a continuing education program. I enrolled, and thus began my many years of sitting in a classroom again.

Since I was an English major, I took an introductory literature course for which the *Norton* was the text. The class met in a dingy room in an old building, typical of what's usually allotted to the humanities, but which I loved because it reminded me of my childhood. The smell of the chalk and the blackboard, the cream-colored walls, the uncomfortable wooden chairs—it felt like home. Once so eager to leave college, I was equally eager to be a student again and looked forward to every class.

One November morning the lecturer, an impassioned young woman, was going line by line through William Wordsworth's long poem, *Ode: Intimations of Immortality from Recollections of Early Childhood.* Gazing out the window, I wondered how the new babysitter was managing. She was a taciturn Polish woman, whom I later found out fed the children a steady diet of pancakes. But I must have been listening at the same time, because I heard the teacher explaining how the poem worked, showing how one image builds upon another until the meaning surpasses the words. It was a revelation to me that words could perform such magic, could become so much more than marks on the page. I thought I knew about poetry, but that morning I felt it with my head and my heart, my mind and my body.

Some of my notes in the *Norton's* Tennyson section date back to that class, but there are none in the margins of "Tears, Idle Tears." I was younger then, with little experience of loss. "Tears, idle tears, I know not what they mean," the poem begins. They "rise in the heart, and gather to the eyes," as the speaker thinks of the "days that are no more." In the middle two stanzas, the poem expands on the image of the tears, until in the last stanza they're transformed into a profoundly human reaction to the simultaneity of life and death:

> Dear as remembered kisses after death,
> And sweet as those by hopeless fancy feigned
> On lips that are for others; deep as love,
> Deep as first love, and wild with all regret;
> "Oh Death in Life, the days that are no more!"

—and so the poem ends. Nostalgia can be a cheap emotion that triggers easy tears, but this poem suggests a profounder reason for it. The language and the imagery have the power to free me momentarily from the prison of self-absorption. Len's and my former life was much pleasanter than our present, let alone what the future may hold, but the poem offers a larger perspective, not by offering consolation, but instead, the commonality of experience.

The poem's last line contrasts the depth of first love with intense regret for what's lost, as if love and regret were inescapably intertwined. It's true; the loss is great and the regret inescapable. Len and I are still together, he's still alive, but it's not the same. It troubles me I can't apologize to him for the words I can't unsay, the actions I can't undo. I'd always thought there would be time, but now dementia has imprisoned Len in another world, and he can't hear me. Time stands still for him while it moves on for me, slowly separating us. There are things about me Len will never know, and things about him I'll never know because he's lost the words to tell me. I regret his loneliness, his not knowing where I am when I'm not with him, his confusion about where he is and what's happening to him. Tennyson's poem suggests the passage of time is death because life inevitably brings death with it, hardly a new thought, but seldom so well expressed. It doesn't say that dementia is a form of death in life.

The older I get, the truer literature seems—it's one of the consolations of old age. I know about regret, as I didn't fifty years ago, when I first read Tennyson in high school. The same is true for music, if on a lesser scale. But I often listen to Mozart's Piano Concerto #21 because I love the *andante* movement. It's now become a staple of dentist office music, but it was less familiar the first time we heard it, which was about when I started back to school. It was incorporated into the score of a 1960s Swedish movie called "Elvira Madigan," a saccharine story about a love affair between a young girl and the soldier who deserted her. Maybe she was pregnant, I can't remember. The movie was filled with gauzy shots of the couple skipping hand in hand through flower-filled fields, while the *andante* played over and over again.

Every time I hear the Mozart piece now, I remember that evening. It was just an ordinary spring night in St. Paul, but perhaps because of the impact of the music, I recall what I wore, what the weather was like and the friends we were with. Then the tears flow for the "days that are no more," for that one day among many that seemed commonplace at the time, and yet is wondrous in retrospect. At least for a moment, my tears seem justified, and I expect there will be more.

XI

The Days That Are No More, Or Life Really Begins

As January progresses, things look brighter to me. I'll always be sad about what's lost, but on the other hand, I'll always be grateful for the memories of Len's and my happier days, even if they only belong to me now. It's ironic that the significance of a moment in time isn't always apparent until after the fact--this seems especially true of travel memories. Away from home, one's perceptions are heightened, and sometimes one's emotional temperature. An extreme form of this phenomenon—hallucinations, dizziness, etc.—is called the Stendhal Syndrome, after Henry Beyle's (Stendhal's) description of his overwhelming physical and psychological response to the Giotto frescoes in the Basilica of Santa Croce in Florence. It seems likely that he was just exhausted and over-stimulated, because I've felt that way myself after a long day of sightseeing in places as evocative as Santa Croce.

Our memories of travel evolve and change over time. What seems significant at the moment—an episode of the Stendhal Syndrome perhaps--fades in importance and is replaced by something entirely different. One of my most vivid travel memories is of the fall of 1958, when Len and I lived in London for a few months while we waited for his two years on active duty in the Army to begin. It turned out to be a turning point in our lives, the full import of which wasn't obvious until much later.

My mother and father were in London for the year and they found us lodging near their flat. Neither Len nor I had spent much time in London and we were so excited about being there that everything was a novelty, even our humble living quarters. We were in one room called a bedsitter, on the ground floor of a three-story red brick Victorian rooming house. Our north-facing room was permanently chilly because the only heat came from a meager gas fire that we fed with shillings and which did little to penetrate the autumn cold. A shabby chintz curtain hid a small sink and a gas ring. When we cooked, which was seldom, the acrid smell of gas blended with the odor of coal smoke still present in the London air.

Len got up first every morning to start the fire and put the kettle on for tea. Following the example of other residents, we kept our few perishables—a pint of milk, a little butter and a jar of jam—on the windowsill. The milkman came by on a bicycle every morning and his bell and the rattling of his bottles were the first sounds we heard as we huddled in bed waiting for the room to warm up. If we wanted a bath, we climbed up a flight of stairs to the common bathroom, soap and towel in hand. The temperature in the little room was Arctic and the only light came from a high, cracked skylight. The rust-stained bathtub was huge, with claw feet and brass taps that emitted a feeble trickle of hot water. In a separate cubicle near it was the W.C., which was also chilly, and which smelled of Jeyes Fluid, a favorite cleaning product in English lavatories. The toilet paper was thin and slippery.

But to us, these inconveniences had the charm of the different. The Spartan plumbing arrangements, however, soon became an issue for me. After a few weeks in London, I still hadn't shaken what we thought were the remnants of a bout of seasickness from a rough channel crossing. An English friend of my parents arranged for me to see a doctor and so one cold morning we found our way to his wood-paneled office on Sloane Street. A stern-faced man in a gray morning coat, the doctor intimidated us both. He didn't seem alarmed, but he ordered tests and told us to come back in a week and when we did, he told us the obvious: I was two months pregnant. Escaping from the office as quickly as possible, we stood on the doorstep in stunned silence, oblivious to the noontime crowds hurrying past.

My parents were equally stunned when we told them the news later that day. By then we had, after a fashion, managed to absorb it. My mother immediately burst into tears, Len and I put up a brave front and my father tried to make everyone feel better by pretending he was thrilled. This seems unlikely, but it was always his nature to be positive. As for Len and me, we hadn't planned to have a baby and the timing was awkward since we would be moving around once the Army took over in a few months.

But we wanted children, it had happened, and the June due date was so far off it didn't seem real. Our ignorance was bliss; we didn't know what we didn't know, and we didn't know much. There'd been an element of chance in our marriage, and now we were embarking on parenthood by chance. The fact that an actual baby was going to appear in a few months was impossible to grasp. I dimly sensed, however, that its arrival would mark the real start of our life. The door to our future had opened a crack.

Soon enough the four of us adjusted to the inevitable and my mother began to consider with some enthusiasm the purchase of small garments, which were especially tempting in London. The trials of pregnancy became more real with the passing days, which were punctuated with unpredictable bouts of nausea. Odors I'd never noticed before took on a new authority, including that ever-present Jeyes Fluid. The pungent scent of curry wafting out the door of an Indian restaurant would send me running for the nearest bathroom, and more than once I had to exit a theater quickly. On one such occasion, I missed most of a ballet starring Margot Fonteyn and Rudolf Nureyev, a loss I regret to this day.

Despite my persistent nausea, Len and I both had a wonderful time that fall. We went to museums and walked for hours and went out into the country. Perhaps we all have what the historian Mercea Eliad calls "holy places," buildings, streets, even whole towns, sanctified by memory. For the two of us, one of those places was the London we knew that fall. It wasn't just the news of the baby that made it special -- it was also the last unbroken period of time we'd spend with my mother and father when it was just the four of us. Our son Ames was born the following June. Soon after, his sister Paris and his brother Nicholas arrived and then there were five of us and it was all so different.

***

Len and I didn't return to London again until many Novembers later, in 1992. By then both our fathers had died, as well as my mother, our children were grown and we were grandparents twice over. We arrived early one dark Saturday morning, weary from the long night flight, and took the tube into the city and our borrowed flat. Once we'd unpacked, I wandered over to a window and looked down at the square below to orient myself. It was a rainy Saturday and there were just a few hardy pedestrians scurrying along the street, their black umbrellas slanted into the wind. We weren't far from where our bedsitter had been, so we'd probably walked through this very square on our way to Harrods or to the Knightsbridge tube station.

The tall, silent white houses looked familiar, as if nothing had changed except the two of us. But any sense of immutability was short-lived. The London of 1958, our London, had almost disappeared, as we learned that afternoon when we set out to find the red brick Victorian house with a front room facing north where we'd lived. Locating the street was easy, but it was impossible to tell which of the refurbished buildings had been ours. Most of them were freshly painted and adorned with colorful window boxes. What had been in 1958 a drab collection of rooming houses and shabby shops was now a bustling upscale neighborhood.

The streets were packed with smart looking couples doing their weekend shopping and the bars and restaurants were crowded. Neither of us could remember the name of the little road where my parents had lived. Tired and dispirited, we wandered listlessly in the wet for a while and then went back to the flat to nap, having given up the past for lost. I was still determined to find some trace of it, but my sense of the gap between London present and London past persisted as the days went by. Len had business calls to make and I was often alone. As I walked the streets and gazed into shop windows, images of our earlier London crowded into my head like guests arriving pell-mell at a party. I felt a mix of pity and envy for our younger selves—we'd had fun, but there was so much we hadn't known.

London was both an album of the past and a reminder of its disappearance. Like our old neighborhood, everything seemed transformed. Gone was the comfortable city we'd known and in its place was a fashionable metropolis. The afternoon before we flew home home, Len was busy and I went to a new play by Harold Pinter, the plot of which centered on the falsification of the past. This was hardly the diversion I was seeking at a moment when I was wrestling with the disappearance of my own. When the play was over, I took the tube to Sloan Square, and started to walk back to the flat. I wanted to window shop, and to savor both the pleasure of being in a foreign place and the freedom of anonymity. It was already dark, but I decided to try once more to locate either our bedsitter or my parents' flat.

Pausing under a streetlight to orient myself, I saw a sign just ahead that said "Pavilion Road," and recognized it as the name of my parents' street. Peering down the long alley, I saw their distinctive triangular doorway. Starting towards it, for a hallucinatory moment I imagined I saw Len and myself—our younger selves--walking towards me, hand in hand, freed from the past. Perhaps we'd knock on the door of the flat and it would open and there would be my parents, returned from the dead, and the world would be as it was before time took it away. It was a true Stendhalian moment.

But if my heart longed for the past, the lure of the present was stronger. I turned away from Pavilion Road and walked ahead into the shadowed emptiness of the adjacent square. I wasn't a girl anymore but a middle-aged woman, tired and cold and anxious for a warm room, a glass of wine, and the man who waited for me. I never told Len I'd found Pavilion Road—it was my moment alone, a fleeting vision and a potent reminder of the simultaneity of past and present, of the myriad ways in which the past informs the present.

That night I was reading *The Leopard*, Giuseppe Tomas di Lampedusa's great novel about Sicily. I'd reached the scene near the end in which the protagonist, Don Fabrizio, watches a young couple waltzing. He finds them "the most moving sight there, two young people in love dancing together . . . deluding themselves that the whole course of their life would be as smooth as the ballroom floor, unknowing actors set to play the parts of Romeo and Juliet by a director who concealed the fact that tomb and poison were already in the script." The Don is right about the tomb and the poison--they *are* always there--but nonetheless, the dancers' illusion is real to them. Their challenge, and Len's and mine at this very moment, is to preserve the intoxication of a moment right up to the doors of the tomb. Wonderful as the past was when we were young and foolish, I was content to be where I was, where we were now. Unlike my younger self, this time I grasped this hour's significance.

In spite of everything that's happened to us recently, Len and I sometimes—at moments--take the same pleasure in each other's company that we did all those years ago as near-children in London. I've read that teenage infatuation is as good a basis for marriage as any, which I find reassuring and based on our experience, believable. Right now, almost every day, the memories of our early years together keep me going. When I look at Len, I see him as he was. He may have lost most of his memories, but he's retained a sense of how it was with us.

Although we left part of our younger selves in the London of 1958, something of those two ignorant children, shivering happily in the bedsitter, is still with us. The way I remember those few months is very different from how it felt at the time, but it's all of a piece. This is what I cling to as January comes to a close.

XII

A Medical History and a Death

However sustaining, memories don't help when our latest medical crisis occurs. One morning in mid-February, an aide finds Len on the floor of his room, disoriented and drooling. He goes by ambulance to the emergency room at Rhode Island Hospital, the largest medical facility in Providence. When I catch up with him an hour or so later, he's already in a cubicle. Confused and angry, he wants to know why he's there--apparently he doesn't remember either the fall or the ambulance ride.

We wait for nearly four hours while tests are done, CAT scan, blood work, etc. Len is left strapped to the hard plastic gurney with his long legs dangling over the end of the bed. He complains bitterly about being uncomfortable, but there's nothing I can do except pester the nurses. Sitting on the hard plastic chair wedged into a corner of the room, I remember the other times we've been here, this way station on the long road of Len's decline.

***

The first time was shortly after New Year's Day 2005. That morning, Len stepped out on the front porch to fetch the Sunday paper and slipped on a patch of black ice on the steps. He fell hard on his back, but other than feeling a little stiff, he seemed fine. Then, over the next few weeks, he seemed to be sleeping a lot and dozing off at odd hours. When I noticed his left leg dragging, I called our doctor and he ordered us here to this very ER. Len was quickly diagnosed with a cerebral hematoma. Because of his pacemaker, he was on a blood thinner and his fall had precipitated the bleed. He was operated on a few days later and the surgery went well. After ten days or so he came home feeling pretty much himself. Perhaps, we thought, life would soon return to normal.

A few days after Len got home, he had his first outing. Ames called us one morning to say us that he and Pascale, who'd been living together, were getting married the next day in a lawyer's office in Providence. (He'd been divorced from his first wife for about five years.) Pascale's mother was visiting from France and it seemed a good time and by the way, did we want to come? We made it, Len dressed in sweat pants and leaning on a walker. I refurbished one of his hospital bouquets so Pascale could have a flower. Their year-old daughter Juliette was with them, and after the brief ceremony we all had lunch in a Thai restaurant. It was a happy occasion and since Len came through it with flying colors, I began to breathe more easily.

A few weeks later we were driving to the hospital for a routine check-up with the surgeon when Len had a *grand mal* seizure. Having never seen one of these, I thought he was dying. We were almost at the hospital, so I sat on the horn, ran a few red lights and pulled up at the door of the ER with screeching tires. Len was carted off and I collapsed in near hysteria. After a seemingly endless wait, a doctor came out to tell me Len was okay. He should stay a few hours for observation, but then we could leave and follow up with our neurologist.

Len was not okay, and as the day wore on he became increasingly agitated, and then one leg began to twitch. Paris and I sat with him, more worried with every passing minute, and more annoyed with the doctors who were paying scant attention to our concerns. By the end of the day, Len's symptoms alarmed even them and he was moved to a ward-like room, a holding tank for patients who'd fallen through the cracks. His symptoms worsened, until finally he was admitted to the Neurological Intensive Care Unit. I trudged back to the parking garage with his clothes in a plastic bag, wondering what on earth we were in for now.

The next day Len was running a high fever and by early afternoon he was incoherent. He was put into an induced coma and we were told he was gravely ill with a mysterious infection. Paris drove me back to Little Compton. It was a miserable night, rainy, cold and very dark. I put on a CD of Renee Fleming, who was one of our favorite singers, but when I heard her voice, I turned the music off. If Len died, I didn't think I would listen to opera again.

Len didn't die, but he was in the coma for about a week while we sat by his bedside. Paris brought in a CD player and we played music we knew he enjoyed, like opera. The machine that fed him intravenously made a constant, quiet gurgling noise and he looked very peaceful. Gradually his temperature fell. He was revived and slowly became himself again. After a few weeks of rehab, he came home and once again, we thought life would return to normal. Once again, we were wrong.

We knew by then that Len would always be subject to seizures, and as the weeks passed there were many of them, some barely noticeable—Len would simply stop and stare into space for a few minutes. Some, however, were worse. Late one September night, right after our 50th anniversary, he woke up feeling odd, as he told me later. He went out into the hall and fell with a crash, knocking over a heavy plant stand as he went down. Waking with a start, I ran out to find him lying on the floor on his back, semi-conscious and with his head in a pool of blood. I called the ambulance and kneeling by his side, begging him to stay alive and weeping into the phone that my husband was dying.

But again, it wasn't as bad as it looked. By the time the ambulance roared into the driveway, Len was waking up from another *grand mal* seizure. The cut on the back of his head turned out to be superficial and by mid-morning he seemed completely himself. He came home from the hospital the next day and after a week or so, the episode seemed like another bad dream. In October, we were able to take a boat trip on the Danube. About a week after returning, though, I noticed Len's leg dragging once again and soon we were on our way to the hospital. A few days later he had a second operation for the hematoma that had resulted from his fall the previous month. More rehab followed, and then another return home.

This time, the signs of permanent damage were more evident and I knew our life had changed. Gradually, Len's absentmindedness and confusion became more noticeable. The seizures continued. Although there were no more *grands mals*, some of them lasted for as long as a few hours. Often one of his limbs would stiffen and he would be unable to move. Sometimes I called the ambulance, sometimes not. Sometimes he was in the hospital for a day or two, sometimes not. There was mention of small strokes. Almost without realizing it, I became the head of the household. We had always handled our finances together— now they were my responsibility, along with just about everything else. And then we moved to Laurelmead and Bridges.

***

Now here we are, back in this familiar ER, waiting for a verdict. I can't tell how sick Len is. He seems better and as the day drags on and nothing happens, we both get increasingly annoyed. When I'm about ready to get Len dressed and leave, the doctor rushes in and with a dismissive wave of his hand, says it's probably "just" bronchitis and Len can go. It's clear he's impatient with chronically ill old people. Just wait, I think, just wait until it's your father or mother.

I get Len into the car and back to Bridges, although he's shakier on his feet than usual. He goes right to bed but seems okay, at least in comparison to how he was that morning. But he's not okay and early in the evening, I get a call telling me he's confused and coughing badly. When I get to his room, I'm shocked by how ill he seems. An ambulance takes him to the ER at Miriam, a smaller hospital than Rhode Island and closer to Laurelmead, and our second wait of the day begins. Len has difficulty breathing and he looks and sounds sicker by the minute. Finally he's given oxygen, which helps some. A nurse has trouble getting a urine sample and I have to help her thread the catheter, which is so painful that Len, who has a high pain threshold, cries out. I wonder out loud why he has to be tortured. Sometime in the early hours of the morning, he's diagnosed with a lung infection of indeterminate origin and admitted. Walking

92

back to the car in the dark, I remember the dismissive doctor at Rhode Island Hospital.

When I return to the hospital the next morning, Len is in a cramped double room. A comatose old man with a tracheotomy occupies the other bed. The machine requires constant draining and makes a strangled noise, like a dying animal. A shrill-voiced aide—it's assumed the old can't hear--is on duty in case one of the men tries to get out of bed. Len is responding well to the antibiotics and seems better, although he doesn't know why he's in the hospital. I'm sitting in a corner trying to knit when the other man's wife arrives. She has a long conversation with a doctor about possible surgery for her husband, which seems grotesque given his moribund condition. I wonder what I would do if it were Len.

While I'm in the cafeteria having lunch, Len is moved to another room where there's no one watching him and he gets up and falls. I return to find him sitting up in bed with a bloody bandage wound clumsily around his head. When I ask him what happened, he doesn't know. Storming down to the nurses' station, I demand to know why he was moved, why wasn't he watched, why I hadn't been called, etc. The answers to my questions are evasive and self-protective, but Len is moved back to his original room with an aide. A CAT scan shows no damage from the fall, but a problem could still develop. It's happened before.

Luckily, Len never remembers the fall and he continues to improve. In a few days he's discharged to the nursing unit in Epoch, which is on the floor above Bridges. He spends three weeks there, supposedly regaining the strength he's lost. Upset about the fall, I pursue the issue with Miriam. After a letter, several phone calls and some help from a major donor to the hospital, the Board of Directors reviews the case. Their report concludes that the nurse on duty at lunchtime decided Len didn't need an aide as much as another patient. Apologies are made, but the episode proves how badly old people are treated unless they have an advocate, and sometimes even when they do.

Len hates being in the nursing unit, which is another unfamiliar place for him. He dislikes the dining room and makes his displeasure known in loud outbursts featuring his now-favorite word, shit. He's unpopular with the regular residents, who glare at him angrily. For a man who's always been so polite, it's a startling change. He talks constantly of going home, by which he seems to mean his room at Bridges. He cries a lot. I sit beside him and hold onto his arm in its familiar red plaid flannel shirt because I can't think of what else to do.

Len's fits of temper in the dining room suggest that while he has some inhibitions left, he doesn't respond rationally to circumstance. Some of this behavior was obvious before, but it's more pronounced since this recent illness. It's a relief when he returns to Bridges, where he is immediately calmer. He claims he likes being back in his room and settles in quickly, but the infection, whatever it was, has left him weaker both physically and mentally.

***

Len's recent outbursts are unhappy reminders of my father's behavior after the death of my mother. By then though, my father had shut down emotionally, and I don't think Len has. For the most part, their dementias have taken a different form. My father's was caused by a brief lack of oxygen during a cardiac arrest in the early 1970s. He was at a Cornell lacrosse game and would have died on the spot if the team doctors hadn't revived him and gotten him to a hospital. Gradually, over the next ten years, he failed, until he was totally dependent on my mother.

Uncannily, history seems to be repeating itself, with the key difference being that I'm able to care for Len, whereas my mother couldn't care for my father after she was diagnosed with leukemia in the spring of 1982. Because my parents could not manage at home, they came to Providence. Len and I flew to Ithaca and brought them back in a private plane. She was to be treated at Rhode Island Hospital and my father would live with us for the next three months. The morning she and I left for the hospital to begin the treatment, I found her and my father in an impassioned embrace, my mother sobbing that their life was in pieces. My father didn't fully understand what was happened, but he looked utterly lost. Then, I could only guess what they were feeling.

Rhode Island is a small state, which explains what happened next. A doctor with pale brown skin and a strong accent greeted my mother and me at the hospital. He introduced himself as Vishram Rege, a name I recognized only too well. A few years before, his daughter Maya, then about 15, and our son Nicholas had been an item. Nicholas, who was a few years older than Maya, went to an alternative high school. He had long blond hair and dressed in ragged t-shirts and tattered blue jeans. Nothing about him would have inspired confidence in Maya's parents. The Rege seniors had emigrated from India in the 1950s and were coping with three Americanized teenagers. Nicholas could hardly have been their idea of a suitable companion for their daughter.

Maya was an ebullient, pretty girl. She was often at our house and Len and I liked her. But somewhere along the line, there was an episode at the Rege house that was the last straw for her parents. She and Nicholas parted, and I didn't hear the name "Rege "again until that morning at the hospital. While we waited for her to be admitted, I told my mother the whole story. We both wondered how Dr. Rege would feel about treating the grandmother of a boy he'd surely been thrilled to see vanish from his life. When he came back I nervously identified myself as Nicholas's mother, he smiled politely, and that was that.

But not quite, because during my mother's long hospital stay, she and Vishram became good friends. He often stopped in to see her after his evening rounds and they talked at length. She was quite secretive about their conversations, but I suspect the topics included rebellious children and grandchildren. My mother, herself a naturalized American citizen, was sympathetic to the challenges faced by the Reges, who'd left their homes to make a better life for themselves and their children. If only she'd known that two of her great-grandchildren would be Vishram's grandchildren.

No doubt my mother also challenged Vishram on his proprietary attitude toward his family. He told her, for instance, that when they left India he changed his bride's name to Lalita, which was easier to pronounce than her original name. He did this without consulting her, which seemed outrageous to my independent-minded mother. Years later, when we were in-laws, Vishram often told me how much he'd admired my mother's intellect and strength of character, and it pleased me that they'd known each other.

The summer of my mother's hospitalization was a long one for all of us. My mother refused to let me bring my father to the hospital--I suspect because it would have been too difficult for her. I was troubled by this, as I wasn't sure he knew where she was, but I didn't have the strength to overrule her. My father was easy to care for, always cheerful and obliging. Occasionally he got lost when he was taking a walk, but he never got far from the house. All that summer I was torn between being with him and visiting my mother, but Len did all he could to fill in the gaps.

***

Right after Len's return to Bridges, Vishram Rege dies. He and Lalita had just returned from their annual trip to India and feeling unwell, he went into the hospital. He was soon diagnosed with liver cancer, and a few weeks later he went home to die. On a chilly morning in late February, I join the Rege family for his cremation. When I walk into the chapel at the crematorium, there's Vishram, lying in an open cardboard coffin that's draped in white and red and gold satin. His hands crossed on his chest, he's in white, with garlands of flowers around his neck. I have an excellent view of the body and although I've never liked open coffins, Vishram's presence in the room seems right. The body's absence makes death seem the unmentionable, when in fact it's the reality of any memorial service.

In the years since Nicholas and Maya married, I've learned that Indian ceremonies don't start on time. They include a lot of what looks like milling about and inevitably run overtime. Unfolding in a seemingly ad hoc fashion, they're subject to revision, long pauses and even long breaks and this service is no exception. The priest, who looks chilly in his white robes, sits cross-legged on a blanket near the coffin. Rice, flower petals, incense, various liquids and a roll of aluminum foil surround him. When he lights a small fire, the attendants from the funeral home watch with admirable aplomb, showing concern only when the smoke threatens to set off the alarm system. After a whispered consultation, they open a door, and let in a blast of frigid air.

The ceremony is long and mostly unintelligible to me, but the idea of sending the dead off properly is universal. When it's over, we circle the body and scatter rice around Vishram's mouth and strew flower petals on his heart. Looking down at his closed, serene face, I ponder what it must be like to live in a strange culture and to die far from the home one may long to return to in death. I think of my mother, born in British East Africa and buried in Rhode Island, and of her friendship with Vishram. One more connection to her has been broken.

We follow the body into the crematorium. I've never been in one before, but it seems better to know what happens than to wonder. Freed of its draperies, the coffin is positioned in front of the open oven. One of Vishram's grandchildren pushes a button and the coffin vanishes into the whoosh of flames that sends the soul on its way. We take a walk in the cemetery and adjourn to a nearby Indian restaurant for lunch. Visiting Len later that afternoon, I don't tell him where I've been. I don't want to know he's forgotten about Vishram's death, which I suspect he has. I like to think I'm protecting him, when in fact it's myself I'm sheltering from the knowledge that he has so little memory.

XIII

Two Birthdays

Vishram is the first one of our children's in-laws to die, a milestone of some sort. Now it's March and winter is finally coming to an end. Len's 76th birthday is on the 18th. When I remind him of it, or each time I remind him, he tries to claim he's only 75, which makes us both laugh. The morning of the 18th is unseasonably warm so we sit outside in the sun for a while, waiting for his two older sisters to arrive for lunch. Len is happy to see them and chatters away during the meal, even though his conversation goes around in circles. He asks them over and over again where they're living. His oldest sister, who was twelve when he was born, tells the now-familiar story of their father announcing the arrival of a baby brother, and how excited he was to have a boy after two girls.

Their visit makes it a pleasant day, more serene than Len's 75th birthday a year ago. Early that January, I'd decided we needed a break from the weather and the stress of the upcoming move, plus which "75" seemed a number worth celebrating. After some thought, I made reservations for a cruise from Miami through the Panama Canal, around Mexico and up to San Diego. We'd never been on a cruise and it sounded restful and doable, even for Len. That I could think so suggests the depth of my illusions about his mental and physical capabilities. I still thought I could keep him safe beyond the confines of home.

The trip was doomed from the start. The day before leaving, we got the results of some tests designed to determine the extent of Len's dementia. He and I sat across the desk from the psychologist while she explained his performance. There was no ignoring the clock face he couldn't draw, the pictures he couldn't complete and the sentences he couldn't finish. Her diagnosis was moderate dementia, edging towards severe. Although she was only telling me what I already knew, I was thunderstruck, and humiliated for Len. He didn't seem to grasp what the doctor was saying, but it was difficult to determine what he understood and what he didn't. I left the office in a state of shock.

We went straight from there to look at an apartment at Laurelmead that had just come on the market. It was exactly what we'd been looking for. With the evidence of Len's decline fresh in my mind, I made a bid in spite of the awkward timing, and then spent the afternoon arranging deposits and completing paperwork. I told myself this was the right thing, but it was nerve wracking to make the decision without Len's help. Our bid was accepted right away, and so the die was cast.

The next day we left as planned. We spent that night at the airport in Boston because our flight was early the following morning. On the drive from Little Compton,

which we'd done a hundred times, Len was already confused
and by the time we got to the hotel, I don't think he knew
where we were or why. The night before a trip, especially if
we were already underway, had always been filled with
happy anticipation but the mood at dinner in the hotel that
night was very different as I was anxious and Len was at sea.
I should have given up and taken him home right then, but I
forged ahead.

We met the tour group in Miami and spent the night
at a motel prior to boarding the ship the next day. In the
morning, we were taken on a lengthy bus tour of the city. It
was hot, and by noontime Len was flagging. By the time we
got to the ship he could hardly stand up, and as we walked
to our stateroom, he collapsed. A steward and I got him to
the cabin and a doctor came and hurried us off to the ship's
infirmary. Len insisted he felt fine and didn't understand all
the fuss, but the doctor thought—as did I--that Len's
symptoms could indicate a stroke. It was clear he wanted us
off the ship and since it was due to sail in less than an hour,
our departure was hasty. Before we knew it, we were in a
taxi on our way to a hospital in Miami Beach.

Thus instead of sailing off into the sunset, we sat in
a cubicle in the emergency room at Mount Sinai Hospital,
our luggage jammed in with us. By then Len was feeling
even more himself, but it was too late--we were trapped in
the familiar routine, the endless questions, the tests, etc.
While he was wheeled in and out, I contacted the tour
company, the insurance company, our family, and anyone I
could think of who could help me navigate a way out of the
mess we were in.

Hours passed and still we sat there. Around midnight, Len was admitted with no conclusive diagnosis, but more tests were scheduled for the next day. He was taken up to a room, the gurney loaded down with all our luggage. I took a taxi to a motel where the insurance people had gotten me a room. It was spring break, so there were no rooms near the hospital and I was nearly an hour away. As the cab drove through the deserted city, I wondered how I'd ever get us home.

The next day was Len's 75th birthday. More tests were done and showed nothing alarming. It was a Saturday and everything moved slowly, but I finally chased down a doctor who had the authority to release Len, who seemed well enough to travel. In the meanwhile, we celebrated his birthday with chocolate ice cream from the cafeteria. Having forgotten we were supposed to be on a cruise, Len was quite cheerful, but all I wanted was to get him home. At last we were set free, with a final diagnosis of dehydration and exhaustion, all of it my doing. We left the hospital after midnight. As we stood on the curb waiting for a cab, I swore I would never again expose Len to the outside world.

Our trip home the next day was endless, with a long stop midway. When we finally walked in our door, I wept with fatigue and relief. I'd found out the hard way that Len couldn't function in the world and I couldn't protect him. The seriousness of his mental and physical condition had been demonstrated at a heavy cost to both of us, but most of all to him. From then on, my goal was to get us to Providence, where I felt Len would be safe. Everything made me nervous, leaving him alone, letting him walk on Meadow Lane by himself, picking him up when he fell. I counted the days until the move and it never occurred to me to wonder if I myself would be happy at Laurelmead.

***

When we bought the apartment, I assumed Len and I would live in it together, but in June, when his condition worsened, the children and I decided he needed more care, and so it was Bridges, for better or worse. Now, nearly a year later and with Spring near, I worry about Len's mental decline just in the last few weeks. He seems more confused and less attached to reality. There are more mood swings— anger one minute, tears the next--and he's declined physically as well. Because it's more difficult to take him out, I make an appointment with a neurologist who will come to Bridges.

The doctor turns out to be a pretty young woman, with black hair, startling violet eyes and a gentle manner. Len perks up when she comes in the room and he responds well when she puts him through some of the same tests he had a year ago, when he was first diagnosed with dementia. There's a big gap between what Len tells her he can do and what he can. Yes he reads, he says, yes he watches TV, but he does neither. I don't believe he's deliberately lying--he assumes he does what he's always done. She thinks his recent lung infection set him back, but his failings could reflect the natural course of the dementia. Does it matter? I suppose not, but I can't help wanting to make it better, even if there's no "better" any more.

I can't tell how much Len comprehends about his condition. I try to maintain an illusion of normalcy for him by living in his world as much as possible. For instance, he keeps asking me if I've paid the golf club bill. He wants, he says, to play golf this summer, even if just nine holes. I assure him it's taken care of, and I don't tell him we aren't members any more. Sometimes he'll ask Paris or me where "your mother" is. He mixes me up with Paris, and thus by "your mother" he means me. Other times he remembers that my mother's dead, although he has a weak grasp of who's alive and who's dead. When he asks me where "your mother "is, I say "but that's me," and he laughs. Time is jumbled up in his head, which I understand. Both my parents and Len's are much with me, even though they're dead. Separating one's inner life from one's outer must be even more difficult with dementia.

Len's tolerance for change is diminishing, especially when he's tired. One night at dinner, I find him seated at a table with two women. He usually sits at "the men's table," as the aides call it, as if we were at a club. Apparently he tangled with one of the other men and they'd been separated. Len doesn't want to be with the ladies. One of the women is crying silently into her sandwich, the bread getting soggier by the minute, while the other picks at a pile of napkins on her lap, mechanically folding and unfolding them. She stares near-sightedly into the middle distance, her face vacant. Eventually she takes up her spoon and slowly eats some soup, most of it dribbling down her bib.

Len pushes his soup away angrily, demanding that it be removed, he doesn't want it, he doesn't even LIKE soup. I persuade him to eat it, telling him he does indeed like soup. Still angry, he asks for and gets a grilled cheese sandwich, which soothes him. At least it looks better than the evening's dinner. The meals arrive from the main kitchen on a portable steam table, so everything is either overcooked or swimming in water. I wonder if the staff cares what the residents eat, or if it strikes them as a losing battle. Playing the cheerleader, I encourage Len to finish the grilled cheese and then I get him chocolate ice cream for dessert. He likes this, and so the meal ends on a happy note.

But after supper, Len gets teary. He says how much he hates "this" for me, and when it's "all over," he'll take me to a jewelry store and buy me something. Then, he adds, we can go back to a normal life. I tell him there's no need to buy me a present. I don't tell him "this" will never be over because this is how it's going to be. I pull out the photo album of our trip to China and point to a picture of us on a boat on the Yangtze. He doesn't remember and he doesn't believe we've been to China, even when confronted with the evidence.

Much of our life has disappeared from Len's consciousness. It seems so sad to me, this loss of memory. Before leaving, I remind Len to look at the picture of the villa over his bed, thinking that maybe an older memory might still be intact. I want him to remember our happy times, nor do I want to know if he's forgotten a place that's meant so much to us. The villa is for me an enduring symbol of our youth, of our faith in the future and our love for each other. Over the years since we first saw it, it's gained so much imaginative truth, which is the most potent truth of all.

XIV

The Villa:
An Embellished Memory

Frequently, our only truth is narrative truth, the stories we tell each other, and ourselves—the stories we continually recategorize and refine. Such subjectivity is built into the very nature of memory, and flows from its basis and mechanisms in the human brain. The wonder is that aberrations of a gross sort are relatively rare, and that, for the most part, our memories are relatively solid and reliable. (Oliver Sacks, in *The New York Review of Books*).

What follows is a recollection of a place and a time. To borrow from Sacks' definition of narrative truth, it's been recategorized and refined. It doesn't always separate what happened from what the memory has become. Truer than a "true" story, it's an essential fiction that sustains me now, when the reality of our life is overwhelming. Like the London we knew in 1958, the memory of the villa is an integral part of both Len and me. Memories change over time and become embellished, just as an abandoned seashell is gradually encrusted with smaller shells. The memory of the villa embodies our earliest years. It reflects the pleasure we took in each other and in doing new and exciting things together. When I was a child, I liked nothing better than to imagine myself as a character in a favorite book. The lives I lived in stories seemed more real than my actual life and they had a special truth all their own, as does this memory.

***

We fly to Italy in early September. It's a night flight, and we wake up to see the rising sun turn the snow-covered peaks of the Alps rosy pink. Gradually, the mountains give way to the green hills and valleys of Italy, and finally to the smoky outline of Milan. After collecting our luggage, we step out into the blazing sun to look for the chauffeur from the villa. He's there, a tall handsome man with a cap in one hand, a red rose in his lapel and an expectant smile on his face. He introduces himself as Augusto.

We are still awkward in our new roles as husband and wife, but Augusto treats us with dignity. He ushers us into an old but gleaming Fiat sedan, stows our luggage in the trunk and starts off for Lake Como. He's a skillful driver, but goes so fast that we slide into each other at every turn. When we reach the city of Como, he leaves the highway for a narrow road that winds along the western shore of the lake. We speed through one village after another. Dogs run for safety and old women in black with net shopping bags press themselves against the high stone walls lining the road. Tantalizing glimpses of blue water appear and disappear between rows of spikey cedars.

At a village square like the ones we've already passed through, the car turns abruptly into a narrow alley, more like a sidewalk than a road. Augusto spins the wheel from one side to the other as we twist and turn on the dirt track that leads up the side of a high promontory jutting out into the lake. Holding tight to the hand straps, we peer over the edge of the road at the dark water below. Augusto points out the shadowy outlines of great blocks of stone just visible beneath the surface. "Pliny," he says, "la casa di Pliny." Later, we learn that in Roman times, Pliny the Younger built a villa on the site and the stones in the lake are all that remain.

A wrought iron gate covered with vines materializes, as mysterious looking as if Sleeping Beauty's castle lies beyond. Augusto jumps out to remove a heavy chain, opens the gate to drive us through, and gets out again to refasten the padlock. The car creeps down a steep hill and there is the villa, its golden stucco walls shimmering in the sun. Above and to the left of the main structure stands a statuesque loggia, an open-sided, arcaded portico with a room at either end. Dense shrubbery runs down one side of the villa to the lake. On the other, gravel terraces alternate with grassy spaces. The terraces are enclosed by stone balustrades, carved with the repeated motif of a baby emerging from a serpent's mouth. This is a *biscone*, the crest of the Visconti's, the ancient Northern Italian family who once owned the villa.

We only know its more recent history. In 1911 Len's great-uncle, a New Englander and a bachelor, saw the villa for the first time. He was with a group of friends who'd been given permission to picnic in the gardens. The house had been closed up for almost 40 years because the French widow, a marchesa, of its Italian owner had fled to Paris after an

108

unhappy love affair. I imagined the uncle, whom I never met, as resembling a character out of a novel by Henry James. Perhaps while his companions rested after lunch, he tried a door or two and found them locked—or maybe he discovered a window ajar, pried it open and explored the empty rooms.

Whatever happened that day, the sleeping villa had found its prince. The next day, he bribed the caretaker to show him the interior, after which he wired an offer to the Marchesa's agent in Paris. It was refused, and then the onset of World War I brought an end to the negotiations. But when the war was over--by then he was married--he tried once again to buy the villa and succeeded. He and his wife were childless and they devoted their energies and their resources to restoring the villa. They summered there every year except during World War II until his death nearly 40 years later. A general in the National Guard, he was always referred to by the staff as *Il Generale*.

The present-day staff is lined up at the entrance to greet us. There are two gardeners with their wooden rakes, a small boy holding out a bouquet of flowers and a pair of girls in blue and white uniforms, who introduce themselves as Emilia and Fernanda. They hurry to get our luggage, but when we try to help they wave us away and beckon us inside. Set in mosaic on the floor inside the doorway are the words, "*Faye ce que voudras*;" do what you will.

And so we do. Each day at the villa begins with the sounds of the gardeners' voices under our window and the maids' footsteps in the hallway. Our needs are anticipated before we know what they are. If we choose to be alone, everyone vanishes; if we're thirsty, lemonade appears magically. There's nothing servile about the staff. From the major domo down to the smallest garden boy, they comport themselves with quiet dignity, lending us the grace we lack. Pretending to be at ease in front of them becomes habitual and we begin to be what we are, husband and wife.

It's a small villa. An interior staircase connects the four levels, each with two or three rooms. On the lower levels are a large living room and a dining room with a red tile floor and long windows looking out over the lake. The kitchen is even lower down, with another small bedroom underneath it. Perhaps our favorite part of the villa is the loggia. It stands on the highest point of the land and from it we can look across the lake to the village of Bellagio and the hills beyond. Years later, this elegant structure appeared on the back cover of *The New Yorker* magazine in an ad for Four Roses Whiskey. It was like seeing one's most intimate dreams displayed on a highway billboard.

We sleep in a bedroom on the top level of the villa. A large room, its walls are covered in gold-embossed black leather. Six long windows look out over the lake and the bed is enormous, with carved mahogany posts and a billowing yellow silk canopy. On the wall facing it, hangs a ceramic plaque of the Madonna and Child, attributed to one of the Della Robbia brothers. This seems as questionable as the attribution to Breughel of a murky oil painting in the living room, but it doesn't matter because it's lovely. Every morning, the youngest and shyest of the two maids brings us coffee in gold and white majolica cups, a pattern made especially for the villa, chipped and faded now, but still beautiful. Flinging open the shutters, she lets in the light. The black walls mirror the sun and the gold of the coffered ceiling reflects the surface of the lake until the room seems to shimmer with light and the scent of wisteria drifts into the room from the gardens below.

We explore every corner of the house. One night, we slip across the hall and sleep in the other bedroom on the floor, which belonged to the general's wife. It's resplendent, with red, blue and green frescoes copied from a house at Pompeii--even the cavernous bathtub is bordered in red and black. On a night when the moon is full, we creep down to the little bedroom on the lowest level, below the kitchen. Lying in bed, we hear the ringing of the bells of the fishing nets on the lake. Kept awake by the novelty of the sounds and the oddity of each other's presence, it's hard to tell which is stranger, being at the villa or being together.

Some days, we abandon our sanctuary to explore the villages around the edge of the lake. Often we take an old mahogany motorboat, polished by Augusto until we can see our faces reflected in the wood. I'm impressed by Len's ability to handle the large craft, while I sit uneasily in the bow. He's been raised around boats and I have not. Under the illusion that what I can't change in him I'll alter in myself, I vow to become a sailor. I never do, but that's another story.

Other days, we board one of the jaunty little steamers that chug from village to village around the lake, their decks crowded with English and German tourists. Occasionally we venture forth on bicycles as ancient and well kept as the car and the boat. Off we go, bumping down the dirt road that leads from the villa, a picnic basket dangling from Len's handlebars. We eat our lunch in one of the village parks dotting the lake's edge. One day we find ourselves next to a party of elderly British tourists, equipped with blankets, spirit lamps and elaborate food. With the arrogance of youth, we claim to prefer our simple repast of rolls, cheese and hardboiled eggs.

It's the 1950s and World War ll seems long over to us. The lake, however, has not forgotten and signs of the conflict are visible. Mussolini was killed in a village on the villa's side of the lake. When we drive there one day, we think we see a smear of blood on the wall in the village square. When we close the gates of the villa that night, we're newly conscious of the shadow of death and destruction that dims the beauty of the peaceful villages, and even of the villa itself.

We're told Germans commandeered it as an officer's billet. The staff took most of the valuables and hid them in the hills so there was little damage, but I wonder if the chipping on the Majolica pottery is evidence of the occupation. The war's legacy is more obvious to us one day when we row to an island in the lake to have lunch at a restaurant managed by a German. We're told he fell in love with the area during the war and returned in peacetime. A big red-faced man in a chef's apron and cap, he passes among the tables with an enormous knife and a wheel of Parmesan from which he cuts chunks. The other patrons, mostly family groups, accept the cheese with polite but distant smiles. When he comes to us, we shake our heads and say no.

Every time we return to the villa from the outside world, it's like passing through a magic curtain into a private universe. On days when we don't want to leave, we look at the faded photographs of house parties and of the Generale and his wife that crowd the tabletops. We peer into drawers scented with sandalwood and lavender and turn over faded linens stored away for years. We leaf through the musty volumes in the marble-floored library that occupies one wing of the loggia--yellowed documents fall from between the pages.

The villa, we learn, has seen its share of murders, poisonings and clandestine love affairs. Chilled by the cold of the stone beneath us, we shiver at the evidence of events so alien to us, we who will always be happy. Then we go out into the sun and lean over the balustrade and watch the boats on the lake come and go. Sometimes we swim before lunch, easing ourselves into the icy lake from the steps of the water gate that is the entrance to the villa for visitors arriving by boat. Warming ourselves in the sun, we inhale the scent of the roses billowing in pink clouds around us, their musky odor intensified by the noonday heat. Cicadas hum as we speculate whose feet might have worn the deep groves in the steps. Cardinals, duchesses, prime ministers? It seems incongruous to be in their ghostly company, two people with no history of their own, from a country with a brief past.

We are served dinner every night on the lowest terrace, just above the lake. A lantern hung from a tree bathes us in a circle of light and the music of the fountain's splashing mingles with the crunch of the maids' footsteps on the gravel. The chef cooks us foods we've never eaten, like *polenta* and *zucchini fiori*, and each night a more elaborate dessert. The low hum of his radio punctuates the sound of the gentle sound of the fish jumping in the lake.

We drink a local red wine so harsh we can hardly swallow it. One night while the maids are in the kitchen, we pour it over the railing and laugh to imagine what it's doing to the fish. After dinner most nights, we climb up to the loggia and sit under its arches, nestled in a double wicker chaise with a deep hood that curves over us. We talk of the years to come and listen to scratchy recordings of long-dead Italian tenors on an ancient machine. (Much later, when we'd come to love opera, I remembered those thin miraculous voices and wondered whose they were.) When the breeze is in the right direction, we hear the faint strains of the band that plays on the terrace of the Grand Hotel Villa Serbelloni across the lake in Bellagio.

On our last night at the villa, Augusto decorates a fishing boat with lights and flowers and rows us out onto the lake. We anchor and drank *prosecco*, a sweet Italian wine that gives us both headaches the next morning. One of the gardeners plays the guitar and sings. Trailing our hands in the water, we look back at the villa on its promontory, the façade punctuated by squares of light. The raised hand of the statue of St. Francis at the boat port, just discernible in the moonlight, seems to bless us. The next morning the gates of the villa shut behind us and we drive away, knowing that our happiness depends on being with each other; it's a beginning.

***

Some twenty years later, the villa leaves the family. Around the same time, we happen—by chance--to see a movie that was partially filmed in its gardens. The exterior scenes are tantalizingly familiar, but when one character goes through the door we know leads to the dining room with the red tile floor, he re-emerges in a *Louis Quinze* drawing room. It's like walking in our own front door and finding ourselves in a strange place.

I used to dream that if we went back to the villa it would be just the same. This will never be, because a supermarket mogul with unusual sexual habits bought it. We

114

were told he cleaned the statuary and "beautified" the interior, and there was a mention of fur rugs. Some years later, it reverted to the Italian government and the gardens are now open to the public on certain days.

Just recently, I saw an ad in a travel magazine for the villa as an "event space"—it has its own website too. Few things in this world ever stay the same, but my memories of the villa are as true and as real as anything I know. What we have left, or what I have left because Len has lost it, is an embellished memory. It's composed of what happened and what might have happened, an imaginative truth symbolized by the print of the rose-covered water gate that hangs over Len's bed in Bridges.

XV

Spring, and a Little Opera

I have to fight the impulse to sustain myself on memories alone, like those of the villa. As spring nears, the days are increasingly fragmented and there's little time for paying sustained attention to anything, even a good book. Besides, I think I've lost my powers of concentration. When I wake up in the morning, the day ahead seems endless, but then time speeds up and it's already night.

Thus the weeks have flown by and suddenly it's Easter, which was never a major holiday in our household. When the children were little, we dyed eggs and provided Easter baskets. For a few years, I produced the traditional meal of ham and sweet potato casserole. I wasn't much in the habit of holidays, with the exception of Christmas, as elaborate observances were not a feature of my childhood. There was many a Thanksgiving when my parents and I dined on a roast chicken because a turkey was too big and there was no family to swell the ranks. Easter was a non-event except for a basket filled with candy, and sometimes a new hat. The Colts, however, marked holidays properly.

Having felt a bit cheated as a child, more in retrospect than in actuality, I tried to follow the Colt pattern even though it made me feel disloyal to my parents. But as the children got older, our enthusiasm waned and Easter dinner fell by the wayside.

This Easter, some Laurelmead friends ask Len and me to have dinner with them in the dining room and so for the first time in years, we sit down to the traditional ham and a sweet potato casserole. Best of all, there's lemon meringue pie for dessert, which has always been Len's favorite. He's in a good mood and announces that he'll be driving soon now the weather's better. He hasn't brought this touchy subject up for a while, but he'll go to his grave determined to get behind the wheel of a car again.

After his first brain surgery and the seizures that followed, he wasn't allowed to drive for six months. Just as the six months would end, he'd have another seizure, and so it went until his driving days were over. Len was a confident and skilled driver, and it was hard for him to rely on our friends and me. He saw it as another sign of his loss of independence, which it was. But to his credit he was an ideal passenger, his impatience revealed only by his twiddling thumbs.

When we get back to his room after dinner, we find another resident wedged into the bathroom, shouting for help. His pants are wet and there's a puddle on the floor, so he must have headed for the nearest toilet when the need arose. I fetch an aide and together we disentangle him, but Len is oblivious to the fuss. He seems hardly to notice the other residents, and usually acts as if he's never seen them before. For a sociable man who's always been sensitive to others' feelings, it's a change. The majority of the Bridges' residents are similarly disinterested in each other. Perhaps it requires all their energy to survive in their individual worlds. They're like fish in an aquarium, peering out through the glass but seeing nothing. Maybe they live in their heads because it's the safest place to be.

Or maybe they can't conceive of a place other than where they are at the moment. Len, for instance, seldom asks me where I've been and when he does, he pays little attention to the answer. When I leave him on Easter afternoon, he asks where I'm going and when I'll be back. He still doesn't understand I'm less than five minutes away--out of sight is out of mind. Where I am when I'm gone is either a mystery he can't solve or irrelevant. He says it's "awkward" for him when I'm absent, an interesting word choice. When I ask him what he means by that, his answer is vague. His ability to explain his mental and emotional states is minimal. Maybe having feelings without the vocabulary to describe them is one definition of dementia.

***

This morning, the morning after Easter, we have an appointment with Len's regular neurologist, a South African by birth. Despite his brusque manner, he's always been kind to both of us and sensitive to Len's situation. This time, however, it seems as if he'd written him off. There's a medical student with him, and he keeps pointing out to her the odd way Len walks, as if he was a lab animal. Len's still a person to me, but to many others he's just an old man with dementia. Maybe there's even something threatening about him; people think if it can happen to him, it can happen to me too.

As we leave, the doctor pulls me aside and asks if I know that he (Len) is going to die soon. I'm too startled to ask him to clarify what he means by "soon," but he makes it sound like nothing less than a biblical prophecy. He goes on to say he'd like me to consider donating a sample of Len's brain tissue for a research project, adding that he asks this of some his more "interesting" cases. Then he hands me a pamphlet and disappearsd, leaving me both puzzled and wordless.

Getting Len into the car and back to his room distracts me and I forget about the conversation until later. What, I wonder, might be especially interesting about Len's case? Surely the causes of his dementia, which is vascular, are routine. After all, he's had two brain surgeries and numerous seizures, as well as possible small strokes. But beyond that, the vision of his head being sliced open to get the tissue is unsettling.

When I go to Len's room later, an aide is cleaning him up after a bathroom accident. He wears Depends all the time now, but his personal hygiene is sketchy. Seemingly unaware of what had happened, he thanks the girl, sounding every bit his gracious self. Then one of the activities staff stops me in the hall to report in a huffy tone of voice that Len had sworn at her. As Paris says, she'd swear at the woman too if she kept trying to enlist her in sing-a-longs. I find myself apologizing, which is stupid—it isn't me who refused to sing. I could have told her that Len has never liked sing-a-longs.

Sometimes in the evenings before Len goes to sleep, I turn on the PBS news program we used to watch together, but he shows no interest in it or in anything else on television. He pretends to know how to operate the remote, but he confuses it with the control for the lounge chair and ends up flat on his back with his legs in the air. When I say it's bedtime, he'll sometimes insist he hasn't had dinner yet, that it's only the middle of the afternoon. If I try to persuade him otherwise, he doesn't believe me. Then, with a sigh, he'll acquiesce and turn the light out, but I can tell he does it just to humor me.

Lately, he keeps saying, "I'm not there, I'm not there," even more than usual. I want to howl with helplessness because there's so little I can do for him. When we go back inside after being out, he often says he doesn't recognize anything and he's more tentative about spaces now. He asks constantly where his room is, even if we've just left it. When he's not actually in a space, it doesn't exist.

A few days after seeing the neurologist, I finally call the number of the brain research project and ask them to send me information. The idea of cutting into Len's head continues to bother me, maybe because I don't want to think about his death, but I'd like to follow through if it helps the research into dementia.

***

This afternoon, a Saturday, I go to "La Traviata," one of the Metropolitan Opera HD simulcasts that began a few years ago. It's a spare production, set on a practically bare stage with an enormous clock on one wall. Predictably, the hands move a few inches at a time as Violetta's life draws to its inevitable close. Wearing a bright red dress, she's played as a party girl, while the chorus, in black, hovers ominously around her. I'm not wild about the interpretation, which is heavily weighted on the side of doom.

The last time Len and I saw a live performance of the opera was about four years ago, in Venice. We were on a tour led by a young American singer who was trying to make a career for himself—the guiding was on the side. One night he took us to "Traviata," staged in a palazzo. The romantic side of the story was stressed and each act was set in a different room. The death scene, for instance, took place in a bedroom, the centerpiece of which was an elaborate gilded bed draped in faded blue silk hangings. The mixed message of the ending—love conquers all but death eventually kills all--seemed reflected in the palazzo's tattered grandeur. The singing was mediocre, but the setting was memorable.

It was nearly midnight when the opera ended, but we couldn't leave until the tide receded because the streets were wet with a minor *aqua alta*, the tidal influx that plagues the city. When we finally set out for our hotel, the water was still deep enough to lap at our feet and the guide warned us that if our socks got wet we should throw them away. As we sloshed along, we passed a house with a plaque affixed to the front, informing us that the American poet Ezra Pound lived in it with his wife after his release in the 1950s from a mental hospital in Washington. In other words, he'd died right there, in that house. Tucked away at the end of a little alley, it looked like a peaceful refuge for a man who'd had such a tumultuous life.

Our hotel was only a short distance from Pound's alley. We were in a tiny room on the third floor, with windows that looked out over the red-tiled roofs of the adjacent houses, one of which must have been Pound's. Each day, the cooing of the pigeons was the gentle sound that woke us up. Lying in bed and listening to them the morning after the opera, I wondered if Pound had heard them too, and if their soft, sibilant chatter made him as happy as it did me. I doubt though, that he would have approved of the sugary version of "La Traviata" we'd seen the night before.

I don't like going to the opera without Len. It meant so much to both of us and the music always brings back too many memories. On the way home, I thought about that trip to Venice. We'd been there together once before, when the two of us, plus Len's mother, took Paris to Europe. That time, we stayed in a hotel on the Grand Canal and spent hours on the balcony watching the comings and goings of the ferries and the gondolas and the cruise ships. But this last time, we'd been there for a leisurely week, with the chance to see parts of the city we'd missed on previous visits. I can't imagine traveling without Len and I'm not sure I want to return to the places we've been together. If it comes to that, I can't imagine life without him anywhere.

XVI

Passing the Time

While we're walking this afternoon, Len's speech becomes garbled and then he suddenly stops in his tracks and I recognize the signs of a seizure. These episodes last longer now and are more debilitating. His doctors have never explained them, but it's assumed they're the result of his brain surgeries. We make it to the nearest bench and after a long rest, he's able to walk slowly back to his room. Still tired and confused at supper, he acts as if we're in a restaurant, complaining loudly about the service and assuring me we won't be back there soon. He's done this before, sometimes claiming the place is worth a second try, or suggesting we order something else next time.

He seems troubled about spending the night in "this room," and points out his lack of the necessities, toothbrush, pajamas, something to read. I show him the pile of untouched books on his bedside table, which seems to calm him. He must think he's in a hotel, or even a hospital. When I finally settle him down, he lifts his head from the pillow to say, "we make a good team," and he hopes we'll go on for many years. He asked me this morning if he could help me pay the bills, because he doesn't like to think of me doing it alone.

Lately he's been especially moody. One morning I found him angrily pacing back and forth in the hall outside his room. He wanted to go home NOW, he said, he'd been shut up long enough. Annoyed by the aide who was trying to engage him in an activity, he muttered loudly that it was all shit. He often claims I'm not giving him "the full story." I keep trying to explain to him why he's in Bridges, although it's always in vain. I KNOW that, he'll counter irritably. I'm sure that at the moment he does "know it," but he can't retain the thought.

The weather is unusually warm and the last few days have been in the 80's. The courtyard in Bridges is open for business, although the so-called garden is pathetic. There are a few derelict pots with last year's geraniums and petunias still in them, but nothing else. The garden beds have been raked and someone has planted a few pansies that will soon die if left untended. The trees cry out for pruning, their leggy branches reaching up for the sun. They're in as much need of light and air as the residents themselves, who have to be coaxed to go out into the courtyard, where they sit in a nervous cluster around the door.

The director of Bridges calls sometimes to say that Len is upset and he wants to speak to me. But when she puts him on the phone he always says he doesn't recognize my voice. He'll shout into the receiver that it isn't me and hang up. I usually go right over, but by the time I arrive he's fine and doesn't remember calling. The aides often tell me he's been agitated. Some of them are better at calming him than others--one of the best is Kate, an old-timer who's often on duty in the evenings, when the residents are tired and cranky. If she's in the dining room at suppertime, things go smoothly. Josie, a sturdy black-haired woman with a rasping voice, is equally reliable. For a while, there was a young man named Nick, but he had issues with the authorities and disappeared. He was good with Len and I miss him.

When Len's in a "going home" mood, he'll suggest we leave right away so I don't have to make another trip to Providence. He's shocked when I remind him we're already in Providence and also, that the house in Little Compton is gone. Why do I say that? Because I don't have the heart to pretend it's still ours. Then he wants to know if I mean the house with the big red barn, and I hear myself saying yes, that's what I mean. I'm afraid if he thinks it's still ours, he'll want to go back even more.

A few minutes later he'll fuss about needing to clean out the barn, which he did twice a year, in the spring and fall. A methodical man, he'd lug the contents of the workshop out onto the driveway. Then he'd sweep up the dust and the bird droppings that had accumulated. He had a pair of blue workman's coveralls that he used for this and for painting. But the chore he enjoyed most was mowing the fields. A few years after we moved to Little Compton, he bought a blue second-hand Ford tractor, and was never happier than when he was on it. As soon as they were old enough, our grandchildren's favorite activity was riding on Big Blue with him. Our oldest grandson remembers being seriously disappointed when we arrived at his house in New Haven one day without the tractor, which he assumed was always with his grandfather.

Now that the weather is better, we take an occasional drive through a nearby cemetery that's famous for its plantings, especially now, with the flowering trees in bloom. Sadly, a frost killed the blossoms on the Magnolias when they bloomed too soon. Crumpled and brown, they're a sorry sight now, like used toilet paper. Len likes to watch the swans that nest along the edges of the river that borders the cemetery. He says they remind him of the swans on the ponds "where we used to live."

***

I'm reading George Eliot's *Middlemarch*, which has managed to hold my attention as nothing else has for a while. I don't recall when I first read it, but there's a note on the inside cover that says, "This is my favorite novel. Every reading yields new delights and new depths. This is probably the fourth time I have read it." It's dated 3/5/04. I've always loved the novel's heroine, Dorothea Brooke, even though my feelings about her have changed. Like any great fictional character, she's open to multiple readings, some of which depend on one's age at the time. For instance, although I still find him inexcusably selfish, I have more sympathy for the aging Casaubon than I did in my teens, when a man his age—somewhere in his forties—seemed impossibly old.

But appealing as she is, Dorothea is not as important to me as Isabel Archer, the heroine in Henry James's novel, *The Portrait of a Lady*. Despite what I wrote about *Middlemarch*, *Portrait* means more, maybe because Isabel is closer in time to me than Dorothea. I have a favorite scene; it's late at night and Isabel is alone in her drawing room in Venice, staring into a dying fire. Sitting there for hours, she confronts the truth about the man she's married, the villainous Gilbert Osmond.

Isabel can't see over the walls of the virtual prison of her marriage, but that night marks the beginning of the self-recognition that will eventually lead her to a life of sorts. Some readers might want to quarrel with that life, with its typical Jamesian compromises, but it's Isabel's choice. It signals her acceptance not only of the implications of her situation, but of the reality of her future. Although our circumstances couldn't be more different, I can't imagine my future either. My prison, which isn't a prison, has different walls, but they loom very high.

XVII
Reading Books

Fictional characters like Isabel and Dorothea seem almost as alive to me as real people. My parents always spoke about books as if they were real, so the boundaries between literature and daily life were—and are--blurred for me. They were apt to point to the resemblances between a friend or a public figure and a fictional character: "He's just like Planty Pall," my father would say about a senator, comparing him to one of Anthony Trollope's political figures. "No," my mother might answer, "he's Phineas Finn all over again."

The behavior of people closer to home was often explained the same way. For instance, I remember my mother complaining unhappily that her sister, who was in the throes of a divorce, was acting like Flaubert's Emma Bovary; it was a painfully accurate comparison. When I began to read, it was thus natural, in a sort of reverse process, to inject myself into the lives of characters. I was especially drawn to lonely little girls, like Mary Lennox in Frances Hodgson Burnett's *The Secret Garden* or Sara Crewe in

Burnett's *A Little Princess*, which led to some serious over-dramatizing of my life as an only child.

Books always vied for attention with the world around me, and the boundaries between the fictional and the real blurred just as they did for my parents, except my responses were less mediated. I remember my mother reading me *Jemima Puddle Duck*, Beatrix Potter's tale of a hungry fox and a silly duck, who was the proud owner of a straw bonnet with blue ribbons. It was afternoon and I was sitting on my mother's lap in the backyard. When she got to the part where the fox plots to capture and eat Jemima, she pointed towards the row of trees bordering the yard. There might be a fox out there, she said in a hushed voice. So real was the image she'd conjured up, that I avoided the backyard for weeks lest I encounter the fox.

My parents read to me until I could read to myself and even after. Both had strong expressive voices, although my mother's was the more dramatic, my father's the steadier. It was a difference that reflected their personalities. Neither of them worried much about the age appropriateness of the books in question. Thus when I was confined to a dark room with the measles at age 10, my father read me Dickens' *Bleak House*. His other choice was John Buchan's adventure story *Prester John*, now considered politically incorrect, but nonetheless a rousing read.

My parents admired writers, so I grew up believing that people who wrote books were in a special category by themselves. This didn't necessarily shield them from judgment, but it had to be taken into account. It might seem obvious that since he was a teacher and a critic, my father would have the last word on literary matters, but it wasn't so. My mother was an impeccable reader, with a keen eye for the shoddy, the second-rate and the exploitive. She was possessed of formidable editorial skills and no infelicity, stylistic or otherwise, escaped her. It was a family joke that she always spotted the hair in the salad or the smear on the teaspoon—so too she ferreted out the dishonest and the sloppy in a text.

My parents and their friends seemed always to be reading or talking about what they were reading. One of their closest acquaintances was a young would-be poet. One summer day he was lying on the lawn, deep in a book. I engaged him in conversation, wanting to know why his name was Reed. Because, he answered, I like to read. This seemed such a reasonable response that I took the hint and went off to bother someone else. After all, I liked to read too. Didn't everyone?

It took me a while to learn that everyone didn't. There was a family history of reading difficulties on Len's mother's side and he didn't read easily. I knew this when I married him, but it didn't seem important. Sometimes I felt sad that something that mattered so much to me didn't matter to him, and I think it bothered him too. But there was so much else holding us together that it was incidental. Len never questioned my need to read, nor did he ever begrudge me the space and time it demanded.

Always in the evenings, and often during the day, I'd vanish between the covers of a book. He never made me feel guilty for this and he never joked about my bookishness, which must have often been annoying. Nor was he anything but supportive when in my early 40's, I went to graduate school, an enterprise that demanded a lot of time and space for reading, most of it stolen from the family. He never complained—far from it, he was my biggest supporter.

When the time came to move to Laurelmead, disposing of our books was a major challenge. One of the twelve volumes in Anthony Powell's serial novel *A Dance to the Music of Time* is entitled *Books do Furnish a Room*. They also furnish a life, and they had furnished mine. Books had filled the rooms in which I grew up. When I was learning to read, I practiced by spelling out the titles on the bookshelves. Some volumes stood out for their color, like the bright yellow binding of Henry James's *The Golden Bowl* or the deep green of *Moby Dick*. Many of those books belonged to me now, still arranged in the same order as on my parents' bookshelves. Our library was a mix of old paperbacks, purchases, gifts and inherited books.

Whenever we moved, I unpacked the books first because they made an unfamiliar place seem like home. When we settled into Meadow Lane, I worried about mildew because we were near the ocean, so the books were housed in two upstairs rooms, which were drier. When my parents died, our library doubled in size with the addition of their books, few of which I could bear to discard. Having them was almost like having my mother and father with me.

I'd take a volume down from the shelf, something like Yeats's or Elliot's collected poems and sit on the floor and read my father's teaching notes, in pencil on 3"x 5" slips. I had to strain to read the faded handwriting. Leafing through the heavily annotated books, I regained the father whose dedication to literature had shaped my life. My mother's maiden name was inscribed on the flyleaf of some of the books, the earliest of which dated back to her college years.

Their library represented so much of what both my parents were that I could stand in the middle of the room and feel their presence.

Because of the threat of mold, by the time we moved I'd sold most of the books of any value. The most notable of these was a signed first edition of *The Great Gatsby*, with the original blue dust jacket. I'd also parted with a signed copy of Nabokov's *Lolita*, the two-volume green paperback edition that was published in France because of the obscenity laws in the US. My parents had smuggled it into the country buried under my mother's underwear.

This final move to Laurelmead required streamlining both our possessions and our books. Len was already in Bridges when the real work of downsizing began and so it fell to me to decide what to sell, what to keep and what to give to the children. It was heartrending for instance, when Len's grandmother's dining room table went out the door headed for the auction block, I was glad he wasn't there to see it. I made some good decisions and some bad, but each one was painful.

I left the library until last, having first measured the shelf space in the apartment. It was roughly twenty-five feet, which seemed very little, although it would turn out to be more generous than I thought. Out went disintegrating paperbacks, novels I'd never read again, outdated travel guides and atlases. When this barely made a dent, I began a frenzy of de-accession—we were starting a new life and, I told myself, there was always the public library. Progress was gauged by the number of boxes stacked up at the end of each day. When the shelves were empty, the books that were not coming with me went off to the local library for its annual sale. I watched them go, convinced I'd done the right thing. It wasn't until after the move that I realized the enormity of my loss.

When I arranged the books I'd saved on those twenty-five feet of shelving, the gaps were glaring. There were none of Andrew Lang's fairy tale collections—the lilac, the green, the blue—I'd loved as a child. They were secondhand editions my mother had found and given me because they reminded her of her childhood. Most of my father's teaching texts were gone too. There was nothing between Hawthorne and Hemingway and I wondered what had happened to Melville. I wasn't wild about *Moby Dick* but still, every one of the missing books had been part of my life and now they were gone.

All that long summer, I'd kept myself sane by looking ahead to after the move, when I *knew* everything would be better; now the move was over and nothing seemed better. The apartment was a strange place with much of what mattered to me gone, my books included. In time, I bought some of the missing titles back, but with no associations attached to them, they were just books.

I did keep the copy of James's *The Golden Bowl*, inscribed by my father to my mother, Christmas 1948. He and I had bought the book at the college bookstore and hidden it in his sock drawer, where my mother found it when she put his laundry away. She never let on, an uncharacteristic act of dishonesty. I still have the worn copy of James Gould Cozzens' novel *Guard of Honor* that my father "read" constantly the last year or so of his life. By then, he'd lost the capacity to comprehend, but he still defined himself by the act of reading because it was what one did.

The other day I opened my old Modern Library edition of Joyce's *Dubliners*, which I'd also kept. On the title page there's a sketch of a wedding dress, probably executed during a class the winter before Len and I were married. Even those vivid stories couldn't divert me from dreaming about him and our future. Now we have no future together, nor can I envision one for myself in this strange place, so unlike the home we loved, so empty of books.

XVIII
Memorial Day

T en Meadow Lane is empty once again. The people that bought it from us have put the house on the market and left town. It looks just the same from the outside, so it almost feels as if it belongs to us again. One day I drive to Little Compton, park in the driveway and walk around the house. Everything looks as it did the day I left. The sweet-scented French lilac I cut back hard a few years ago, the rusting outdoor shower, the indentation in the ground where the dog run was, they're all there, all unchanged. Len and I are so altered that it seems the house should be different, but no, it's as if time stopped last September.

The daffodils are at their peak and I pick an armful to take back to Providence. I go around the house a second time, keeping a safe distance between it and myself so I can't see inside. It's tempting to imagine us still living there, and sad to know we aren't. Recently I came across a passage in *Falling to Earth*, a new novel by Karen Southwood, which describes this better than I can:

She'll tell him when he stands in front of this house as a man he'll be overcome with the certain feeling they are all still inside. His whole family, waiting for him. It will seem like more than he can bear, the feeling that every moment of his life is still taking place and that he is nonetheless powerless to see it, forced to stand outside with no way in....

Memory is something more than recollection [and] the idea of a moment can sometimes seem as real as the moment itself. I stand outside our house and our life, but there's no way back in. Memory is more than recollection, and what I remember about living in our house is as real to me as when it happened. Len's memory is a jumble, so maybe I'm making up for his loss.

***

Sometimes Len talks about having moved "here," but he seems to mean Little Compton and not Providence. He confuses his memories of his father working in his garden with doing the chores around our house. The two men were very close, and it's as if they've become one person to him. I understand this, as there are times when I feel as if my mother is part of me, when I go by a mirror and see her face reflected in mine. Maybe it lifts Len's spirits to remember he was once a functioning person with things to do, like his father. But he seems more lethargic every day and it's harder to get him out of bed and moving. At moments his speech is slightly slurred and his mouth moves oddly. He keeps asking me--half seriously--if I have a secret life, laughable from my perspective, but perhaps not from his.

There are lapses in the care in Bridges. One morning when I went in, he hadn't been showered and there was no top sheet on the bed. I retrieved one from the tangled pile of linen in the laundry room and finished the job. I've given up complaining to the aides about something so minor. Len isn't bothered, so why waste my energy? But one morning this week there was a hematoma on his forehead, dangerously close to his left eye, and an impressive bruise on one leg. He must have fallen against the bureau going from the bathroom to the bed. He claims he doesn't get up at night, but he does, which worries me because of the potential for falling.

Len gets angry when the aides bathe and dress him. If I try to shave him he pushes my hand away, and one morning the razor ended up on the floor. His outbursts don't mean anything, but they're so unlike him that it's upsetting. I shouldn't try to shave him, but I can't stand the Hitler-like black shadow that grows on his upper lip. Maybe his skin is getting more sensitive, or maybe he hates admitting he can't take care of himself. I want him to look well groomed because that's how I think of him, and I think it's what he'd want. I feel him slipping away, a little each day.

The other residents in Laurelmead are very kind, but we don't share a past and we have little in common but the present moment. Most of the women are widows and many of them have nursed an ailing spouse, so they know what it's like. If we'd stayed in Little Compton, I'd have friends, but I wouldn't have the children nearby, which seems more important now, both for Len and for me.

The decision to move here sometimes feels to me like a retreat and maybe it was the coward's way out. I've been having bad dreams lately. I wake up around 3 AM and toss and turn before falling back to sleep for an hour or so towards dawn, which comes earlier now. That's when I dream the most. I see myself carrying Len's limp body through a crowd of people, crying out for help. But everyone ignores me—they keep telling me that he's already dead. I wake up with a start, exhausted.

Some friends from Little Compton stopped by for a visit earlier this week and I brought Len over to the apartment to see them. Even the short walk from his room is too much for him now and we use a wheelchair. I fed him an early supper because the three of us were going out, but it was a disaster. The tremor in his left hand is worse and he knocked over a full glass of cranberry juice, which upset him and thus me. He recognized our friends, but couldn't carry on a conversation despite their efforts to engage him. Every time I went into the kitchen, I could hear him asking where I was.

There was a piece in today's *New York Times* by the wife of a man with dementia that struck a chord with me. She writes of spending countless hours caring for him at his nursing home. She wishes they were home again, but adds that she aches "for him to be back as him," and there's the rub. Sometimes I lie down on the bed with Len, and it's just the two of us for a moment.

The article ended with a quotation from an EE Cummings poem that husband and wife both loved, called "I carry your heart with me (I carry it in]." I looked it up and found the usual Cummings mix of tortured syntax, odd punctuation, etc., but the image of a heart carried within a heart struck home. Here's the poem:

I carry your heart with me (I carry it in
My heart) I am never without it (anywhere
I go you go, my dear; and whatever is done
By only me is your doing, my darling)
                              I fear
No fate (for you are my fate, my sweet) I want
No world (for beautiful you are my world, my true)
And it's you are whatever a moon has always meant
And whatever a sun will always sing is you

Here is the deepest secret nobody knows
(here is the root of the root and the bud of the bud
and the sky of the sky of a tree called life; which grows
higher than the soul can hope or the mind can hide)
and this is the wonder that's keeping the stars apart

I carry your heart (I carry it in my heart.)

People sometimes ask me if Len's dependence on me
is a burden. At times, yes, but it's also rewarding to feel so
needed. He's been reduced to his essence as a man and
what's left are his honesty, his straightforwardness and his
lovingness, the qualities that drew me to him in the first
place. I might feel differently if I couldn't walk away every
night knowing he's safe--I harbor no illusions about my
shortcomings as a caregiver, a word I've come to loathe. I'm
not a patient person and there were times during our last year
at home when I lost my temper, followed by intense feelings
of shame and regret.

***

Today was Memorial Day, the first long weekend of the summer, and I wanted to be in Little Compton, especially since it was a lovely day. Instead, I went to the movies with two women from here. We had dinner afterwards at an Asian restaurant. Primarily a take-out place, it was hot and noisy and it didn't have a liquor license, so I couldn't drown my bad mood in a glass of wine.

It seemed so dreary, three widows alone in the midst of the happy, laughing groups, and it wasn't even a very good movie. I felt guilty I wasn't with Len, but when I saw him later he didn't mention my absence. We sat in the courtyard and talked about Memorial Day in Little Compton, which he claimed to remember, and perhaps he does.

XIX

Summer

I returned yesterday to Laurelmead after spending two nights with Rhoda and Allen on Cape Cod. It was rejuvenating to be near the ocean again and to look out at the salt marsh in front of their house. I felt as if I could see clearly for a change. My apartment here faces west, but the treetops cut off the horizon just where it begins. Because it's the end of June, the Cape was still quiet. It was a relief to be with good friends who need no explanations.

They may think there's nothing to be done for Len and me, but not so. I can't imagine getting through this past year without the support of the treasured few who've listened and listened, and then listened some more. Rhoda and I met over thirty years ago, when we were both "older" graduate students in the English department at Brown. We both heard about each other-- people in the department kept telling us we should meet. When we finally did, it was almost love at first sight. In the twenty plus years since then, we've been through a myriad of major life events together, weddings, graduations, births and deaths. It even turned out that our husbands had gone to grammar school together, which cemented the friendship.

This was my first time in Wellfleet without Len. It was hard to be there alone, and I was glad to see him when I got back in the late afternoon. He immediately began saying he wants to go home. Once again, I asked him what he thinks of when he thinks of home, not to test him, but because I wanted to come up with a response that made sense. "When we were happy," he said. "Home" is a state of mind to him, which is logical if he's forgotten the actuality of the house.

He's right too-- "home" *is* as much an idea as a place. He didn't seem to realize I'd been away. His left eye looked off kilter to me and he insisted it was time for breakfast, not supper, and complained he hadn't had his coffee. Coming back into his world after being away even for a short time, is never easy. I know every step of the walk between the apartment and Bridges. Seen with fresh eyes, it looked more isolated than usual this morning, more like a holding tank for the abandoned.

When I got there today, Len was in the living room sitting next to one of the women residents, which was unusual as he seldom leaves his room now. She was hugging a large stuffed bear and he was talking to it—the bear--animatedly and chucking it under the chin. A maintenance man walked by and Len, pointing to him, told the woman he could be hired to help out at a cocktail party. She thanked him for the tip, but didn't think she'd be entertaining any time soon. They conversed for a while, each in a separate universe but connecting on some level. Such sociable exchanges are rare, as few of the residents interact with each other, least of all Len. He doesn't remember, but we knew the woman with the bear when we lived in

Providence. It's possible they recognize something similar in each other, like the possibility of hosting cocktail parties.

Marie, one of the more withdrawn residents, was snoozing in a wheelchair next to Len. I was surprised to see her, as she hardly ever leaves her room. She's on dialysis and her skin is the color of a stale lemon. She has an artificial leg with a white sock and a black shoe on it, very macabre. Once in a while she disappears for a few days and then reappears. No explanation is given for her absences, or for anyone else's. It's as if the residents don't exist if they're not visible. Some of them never disappear, like Ozzie, who's been at Bridges for two or three years. At first glance, he seems normal, but he gives himself away by asking every five minutes when the next meal is. Once at the table, whatever the meal, he takes a few bites and then hurries nervously out, like the White Rabbit.

Another old-timer is David, a tall thin man, always impeccably dressed in a blue blazer, grey flannels and a shirt and tie. Every weekend, his harassed-looking son takes away the dirty shirts and returns clean ones. I've been told David taught business at one of the local colleges. Then there's Virginia, who's toothless and hairless unless the aides remember to put her wig on and/or put her teeth in. Mostly comatose, she's capable of some astonishingly coherent remarks. Usually, though she just mutters, "I can't do it, I can't do it."

One of the younger residents is Francesca, who must have been a beauty. Her room is elaborately decorated with art deco mirrors and artificial plants. When Len first moved in, she'd roam the halls, crying and hugging anyone who went by, but now she's in a wheelchair, hunched over a piece of fabric to occupy her restless hands. Her eyes are seldom open and her once dyed hair is growing out grey. She has a private aide who puts elaborate make-up on her, making me think of Miss Havisham in *Great Expectations.*

The director Cindy has just reorganized the unit's furnishings, as if by doing so she can reanimate the residents. Artificial flowers have been brought out of storage and pictures of kittens and puppies hung on the walls. She's also rearranged the furniture, having resurrected pieces that look as if they'd been put away for a good reason. The most unfortunate of them is a gold couch that's low and slippery. Len got stuck in it the other day and was hauled up by Brittany, the young woman who leads the daily exercise classes.

Brittany is a pretty girl with enormous patience who coaxes along her unresponsive audience, undeterred by their propensity to nod off or resist her efforts. Len never fails to label whatever she's doing as stupid or worse, but she teases him until he agrees to play balloon volleyball or a TV bowling game. He's quite good at both of these. He usually insists I play too and he always gets a better score, as he always has. When Brittany first came, she had long blonde hair, but the other day she showed up brunette, with eyebrows dyed to match.

I was glad to see the courtyard has been replanted with new shrubs and flowers, all in one afternoon. Paris was there when the workmen descended on the garden, and she claims she heard their shovels hitting rock, which is not a good omen. The smell of new mulch is overpowering, but the residents seem pleased. A few of them have even ventured out, although they stay clustered around the door, as if frightened by the fresh air.

***

It's been hot and I'm still having trouble sleeping. One night this week the phone rang around 1 AM. It was the wrong number, but the damage was done and I was awake for a long time. Len's youngest sister called me the next morning to say goodbye before going off to Europe. She was the first person I'd spoken to that day and I had to fight back the tears. I envy her the freedom to travel, which is irrational—why should everyone else be stuck just because I am? She assured me something good would come of "all this," but it's hard to imagine what that could be.

The day got better when friends came for lunch, a welcome diversion for both Len and me. We ate in the café over here. Len put on his usual show of perusing the menu until I suggested the cheeseburger, which is what he always orders. I was glad to see him enjoy a decent meal for a change. After the friends left, Len started talking about not feeling "right." He should be able to focus better, he said, and if his father were alive, he'd scold him for not taking better care of our property. If I keep on this way, he said, you'll have to put me in a nursing home--I didn't know whether to laugh or cry. He doesn't seem to notice that almost everyone in Bridges uses either a walker or a wheelchair. At dinner the other night he stared at his meal and announced he couldn't put "it" together, but I didn't know whether he meant the food or his situation. He complains his mind isn't "engaged," and he doesn't know how much more of "this" he can handle.

I wonder if he remembers his mother was in a nursing home at the end of her life. Every time we visited her, he'd say if this happened to him, I should shoot him. Yet neither of us really worried because we thought we controlled the future. Whenever Len forgot something, he'd say half-jokingly, that he hoped he wasn't getting Alzheimer's. My stock answer was that he was too old for the early variety, and there was no history of it in his family. Little did we know.

Lately I've noticed scratches on his face and neck. At first I blamed them on the aides' imperfect shaving techniques, but I'm beginning to think they're self-inflicted and I wonder if it's a sign of anxiety.

***

Ames turned 53 last week. He was born on June 21st, the official start of summer. This year it was a sunny, clear day, just as it was when he was born. I was living with the Colts in Little Compton. When our six months in El Paso ended, Len was assigned to a Nike missile base—already obsolete—in New Jersey. I was 8 months pregnant and our families didn't want me to have the baby in a strange place, so I was sent to the Colts. This was nonsense, but Len and I didn't know enough to protest. He drove up to Rhode Island every weekend and luckily, June 21st fell on a Sunday. Len was able to take me to the hospital and see Ames for a few hours before heading back to New Jersey. Six weeks later, Len drove the baby and me to the apartment he'd rented in Plainfield, a commuter town about an hour from New York. We had two small bedrooms, a pink-tiled bathroom and a living room. There was a fire escape off the kitchen where we kept a laundry rack and a Scotch Plaid grill. We thought of it as our first real home.

Sometimes, now that it's warm, Ames brings his six-year-old-daughter Juliette to swim in the pool at Laurelmead. If it's a nice day, I wheel Len to the adjoining patio so he can watch her splash around. One day, he looked closely at her and out of the blue, told her he hoped she'd be happy. I'm not sure if he knows exactly who she is, but he recognizes her as one of the family. As the youngest of the grandchildren, she will hardly remember him.

Yesterday I went to the funeral home to do the paperwork for the brain tissue donation. It felt weird to make arrangements for Len's death while he's still alive. "The body" will be taken to the hospital before going to the funeral home, so it all has to be set up ahead of time. The man I spoke with joked about what happens at the ER when they arrive with a corpse, which didn't struck me as funny. When he asked if I wanted to "pre-pay" for the cremation, I declined.

I also declined to "pre-arrange" my own funeral arrangements. Maybe this rather bizarre exchange is what brought on another night of confused dreams. I dreamt we were in Pittsburgh, where we lived briefly at the end of the 1960s. Everything about it—our house, the neighborhood, us--was distorted. Len was dying again, but the nightmare was that this time, I wanted him to die.

A few days ago I went to Little Compton for a friend's 75th birthday party. It was the sort of conventional summer gathering Len and I wearied of as the years went on. The summer season is just getting underway and the chatter was all about everyone's winter and what their offspring were up to, and it was so noisy I had to lip read. A few people asked after Len, but not many, which reminded me of my miserable New Year's Eve. It made him seem non-existent, which he is except to his family and a few close friends. I spent the night with a woman whose husband died a few years ago and we compared our respective roles as caregiver and widow. She says she pities me because "the death" is still ahead. I'm re-inventing myself, she says of me, while she insists she just plods along, a simplification with some truth in it—although "plodding along" is a victory in itself. Her husband kept his mind until he died and she's still in their home, which I envy. I took a long walk on the beach. It was a beautiful day and I hated to leave.

***

Once a month I take Len to get a haircut and today was his appointment. It was difficult to get him up the steps, into one chair and then another and then back again into the car. On the way home, he asked me if it would be a problem—he hesitated over the word—to go to Boston to the theater or a museum and perhaps lunch. Maybe, he added, we could even spend the night at a nice hotel. As gently as possible, I said it might be difficult and he agreed, but with a sigh.

For a while after moving to Bridges, he talked a lot about taking a trip or doing something fun. Now he seldom does, which both saddens and relieves me. He doesn't mention playing golf any more or swimming or working around the property, so maybe he understands his situation, albeit unconsciously. Before he turns out the light at night, he talks to the stuffed West Highland terrier I bought him after he admired his neighbor's stuffed dog. Years ago, we had a West Highland Terrier named Bedelia, whom he loved dearly. The toy version sits on his bedside table so he can see it when he wakes up. Sometimes he addresses it as if it were a cat.

XX
Mid-Summer

Hard to believe, but it's already July. This past Sunday, I went with an assortment of children and grandchildren to watch the America's Cup Race trials in Newport, off Fort Adams. Laurelmead seems stifling sometimes and it's a real pleasure to get out into the world. The boats were bizarre constructions, very high tech, nothing like the classic yachts of twenty years ago that I remember from earlier trials. There was a big crowd and it was very festive, with music and vendors of all kinds. As we waited for the races to begin, Nicholas talked about going out with Len on a Coast Guard cutter to watch the races when he was a little boy, and what fun they'd had together. I was glad he was on hand today to explain what was happening when the boats went tearing by us at what looked to me like hull speed.

The last race was abruptly cancelled when the weather turned threatening. Sure enough, just as we lined up for the ferry back to the mainland, the heavens opened, thunder roared and streaks of lightening shot across the sky. We squeezed into a crowded launch and went leaping and bouncing across the open water. We made it, but our clothes had to be wrung out before we could get into the car. I was so tired when I got back to the apartment, my legs were wobbling. I didn't tell Len about the day. He has difficulty picturing things, so I've stopped. My life goes on, his doesn't.

***

I stayed in Providence over the 4th, which dawned rainy and sticky. At lunch, Len said he wondered how we were going to "make it" and I tried to cheer him up. It used to be the reverse, because he was always the one telling me to look on the bright side. When we were sitting in the courtyard, I pointed out a chipmunk, who was hesitantly scouting out the birdfeeder in an amusing way, but Len couldn't focus. Maybe he doesn't see clearly, or perhaps he can't align what he sees with what we're talking about. The weather cleared, so in the evening I went with Paris and her family to see the fireworks display at Providence's new waterfront park. There were families everywhere, spread out on the grass with their picnics. Every ethnic group in the city seemed represented. When the sun finally went down, the fireworks were shot off out over the water, which was spectacular. I was tired when I got back, but thankful for another chance to be somewhere other than in my apartment.

I've been reading some poetry. One of my favorites is Auden's "Musée des Beaux Arts." It's a meditation on Breughel's painting The Fall of Icarus, which depicts the unfortunate winged boy's fall into the sea. The disaster goes unnoticed by the crowds of people on land, who also don't seem to notice Mary, Joseph and the baby Jesus, off in one

150

corner of the canvas. "The Old Masters," the poem says, were "never wrong about suffering." They understood its "human position," and knew that it occurs while "someone else is eating or opening a window or just walking dully along." It's human nature to ignore the extremes of human experience until something happens to remind us of them. Everything happens to nobody, I read somewhere.

Len questions every aspect of his daily routine, even something as minor as buttoning a shirt. He's always checking to see if he's doing whatever it is the right way. Paris says he's grasping for cognition, and gasping for breath too. Just bending over to fasten the Velcro fasteners on his sneakers winds him. He says he likes it when it's just the two of us, and he tries to express how he feels about us being apart. He's always relieved to go to bed, maybe because then he knows where he is and can look forward to a few hours of oblivion. He says he stays in bed until I arrive in the morning, even though he doesn't. The aides say he wakes up in the night and wanders around and I wonder if he's trying to find someone to tell him where he is.

***

Ames called a few days ago from the ER at Rhode Island Hospital and announced he'd had a bike accident. His front tire caught on a crack in the street and he went over the handlebars, which resulted in a fractured tibia and left elbow. I heard him out with composure but later, when I went out in the car, I turned the wrong way on a one-way street, right into the oncoming traffic. My mind must have been distracted by what could have happened to Ames. I didn't tell Len about the accident, as it would have upset him. I used to feel that nothing had really happened until he knew about it, but now I feel I have to protect him. Also, it's too much trouble to explain sometimes.

It's getting even harder for me to manage his wheelchair, especially getting it though a doorway or over a bump in the sidewalk. Len's oldest and best friend Hilary, whom he's known since they were boys, comes for lunch every week and he helped me with it today. He used to take Len out, but now he brings food and we eat in Bridges. Today, Len talked about trying to get together with a mutual friend and fellow classmate at Salisbury. When we reminded him the man's been dead for some years now, Len said of course, but went right back to the subject a few minutes later. He also kept mentioning his parents, saying how much he looked forward to seeing more of them this summer. It must be nice for him to think they're still alive.

Earlier this week I took my first swim of the season in Little Compton. I waited until late afternoon when the beach was deserted so I wouldn't have to talk to anyone. The water was clear and calm, the sand was still warm and the late afternoon sun turned the rocks brilliant shades of red and gold. I sat there for a long time, remembering the long hours on the beach when the children were little.

Once the grandchildren began to arrive, we had a beach picnic at the end of every summer. It was a job to lug everything across the sand and build a fire. Too often the wind was blowing, and more often than not, the children were cranky. But those were precious times, sand in our faces, gritty hot dogs and all. I remember the year we knew that Paris's husband Henry had colon cancer. While we were building the fire, I looked up and saw him standing high up on the rocks and staring out at the ocean. I thought he might be wondering if he'd be alive in a year, as I was. He died the next July and we had our picnic without him.

***

Len announced this morning that he needed a new pair of Levis for his garden work. I don't know what prompts these memories to reappear. He seemed distanced at lunch and complained the food tasted bitter and that all he does every day is eat breakfast, lunch and dinner. I helped the aides serve lunch because they were shorthanded. It's quite a job to get everyone into the dining room and there's often a drama because someone sits at the wrong table or wanders off.

While I was handing out the soup, Virginia interrupted her nonsensical monologue to ask if I was training to be a nurse's aide. In the afternoon, I took Ames shopping at a very crowded Whole Foods because he can't manage it alone with his injuries. His son Alex, age 16, was with us, and he wasn't in a helpful mood. He was delegated to push the cart while I dealt with Ames's wheelchair, but as we worked our way through the narrow aisles of the produce section, Alex "lost" the cart, and I almost lost my temper. Before we were done, Ames had food stuffed in all around him.

I noticed tonight that Len has a tremor in both hands now, although it's more severe on the left, his weaker side. He keeps murmuring, "It's hard, it's hard," and "I try," I try." We tell him we know it's hard, except we don't, not really. When I was getting his dinner, the aide in charge shooed me away. An officious woman with a shelf-like posterior, she insisted that only staff was allowed near the food and no one was to be fed until all the residents were in the dining room. Neither of these policies had been enforced before. Finally she handed me a plate heaped with food, far more than Len could eat. When I got back to the table, his left hand was waving in the air and he was talking nonsense. It looked to me like a seizure, so the aide gave him some medication she said would "calm him down." Heaven knows what it was, but it seemed to work. After ten minutes or so I was able to feed him. He ate like a little bird, opening his mouth for each bite.

We made it back into his room, but he collapsed on the floor just short of the bed. A shy young Black woman who is new to Bridges answered my call for help, and she knew exactly what to do. First she got Len to put his arms around her neck and then she swiveled him onto the bed. I didn't even try to persuade him to brush his teeth, which is a challenge on the best of nights. When I left, I looked back through the crack in the door. Len was lying on his right side with one arm flung over the opposite shoulder, which is how he's always slept.

Our first bed, in Middlebury, was a maple four-poster. We had a pink-and-white-nylon-puff my mother bought on sale as part of my "trousseau." A few years later, Len's mother gave us a king-sized bed with twin mattresses because she considered a good bed essential to a good marriage. We slept in comfort from then on, with plenty of room for a cat or two. Now the cat and I sleep in a full-sized bed that was in one of our guestrooms. Paris has our bed, and one night I slept in it, on my old side. It felt very strange.

***

I'm reading Richard Ford's new novel, *Canada*. Early in the story, the main character/narrator recounts a rare good moment in the life of his ill-matched parents:

It was as if they'd discovered something that had once been there but had gotten hidden or misunderstood or forgotten over time, and they were charmed by it once more and by one another . . . . They caught a glimpse of the person they fell in love with and who sustained life.

I still catch a glimpse in Len, even now, of that boy who came down the stairs into the living room at Emma Willard. Later, a character in the novel remarks that once in a while, a word you've heard forever "all of a sudden makes a whole different sense." Love means something different to me now than ever before and so does the idea of loss, the prospect of which seems to sharpen love. The same character also claims "Life's passed along to us empty. We have to make up the happiness part." To the extent that we have to make the best of what we're given, that's true, but some of us get more to work with than others—I count myself among the lucky ones who've been given a great deal.

Len's anti-depressant dosage has been upped because of more frequent outbursts of agitated behavior or "aggressive episodes," as the director calls them. I feel as if the man who behaves this way isn't Len, but a force that momentarily possesses him, and the old Len, the true Len, always returns. He asked me the other day if I'd brought him "here." He wanted to know if being "here" was part of the "process." Often he just stares into space, his head bent forward. It's more difficult to rouse him and the children and

I end up talking around him. A couple of times lately he's asked anxiously if I have a "secret admirer." I tell him I'd like to know who that could be. Does he have any candidates?

His face looks more rigid on the left side and he seems groggy and I wonder if he's had a mild stroke or two. When I'm with him, he wonders out loud where I am if I'm not in his direct view. He talks about adjusting to the "new regime," whatever that means, whether it refers to where he is or how he feels is hard to say. He acknowledges he can't go swimming now, but maybe later in the summer. I wonder if he really believes he's getting stronger, or if it's his lifelong optimism talking. But he also claims he's discouraged because he doesn't see his physical condition improving.

***

One of the female residents in Bridges had a birthday the other day and I arrived to find everyone around the table in the living room with party hats on. The director was trying to get them to sing with her, and she complained to me that Len wouldn't come out of his room, even when promised birthday cake. Cranky Margaret was part of the group and looked especially silly in a pink paper bonnet to which she seemed oblivious.

At dinner that night Len announced in a loud voice that he'd never had an affair—where that came from, who knows. Honestly, I don't think either of us could have survived the turmoil of an affair—order and loyalty were too important to us. A friend once told me that she knew when she walked down the aisle that the marriage was a mistake, but she decided it was okay because she could get a divorce, which she did. Our marriage hasn't been perfect, but it's been a lot better than any alternative I can imagine. Perhaps it was never put to an extreme test, although just living together for a long time is challenge enough. In sum, I can't imagine living with anyone else.

Len's legs tend to give way underneath him now and a few times we've come close to collapsing together in a heap on the floor. Once an aide rescued us from a disaster in the dining room by putting a chair behind Len just in time. Almost every night, either Paris or I—whichever one of us is there—have to straighten him out on the bed before we leave.

XXI
Making Do

The days drift by, and suddenly August is nearly over. This morning when I ask Len how he's feeling, he responds that he's not well, not well at all. He's worried because the sales figures are down and the numbers look grim. He goes on in this vein for some time, while I try to figure out what he means. It doesn't take long to realize he's reliving the biggest blow of his business career, the failure of Bruin Box, the packaging company he bought in 1971, when he left Reed & Barton and we moved back to Providence.

Len threw all his considerable energies into Bruin, but after about twelve years of progress, the competition from China put too many of his customers out of business, and Bruin followed. All I could do this morning was to assure him things would get better. Eventually he calmed down and his restless mind moved on, but the resurfacing of Bruin all these years later was proof of how disturbed he was by its failure. He always worked so hard at everything he did, convinced he could make success happen.

He should never have blamed himself for Bruin's demise, as there were too many forces arrayed against him. But he did, and fell into a deep depression around the Christmas of our first year of living full time in Little Compton. We'd extended ourselves financially to build the house and our future looked pretty insecure when Bruin failed. Len was such an optimist that I thought he was immune to gloom, even then. Yet ironically, I realized over those dark winter months that whenever he came in the back door whistling, it meant he'd had a bad day; he whistled to spare me his distress.

One moment from that time stands out. We'd quarreled about something minor and Len, who was undressing, grabbed one of his shoes and threw it hard against the wall. I'd so seldom seen him angry that it took my breath away and I retreated from the room in a state of shock. I don't think I ever managed to convince him that the loss of Bruin mattered to me only because it was a disappointment for him, and not because I thought he'd failed. As I listen to him this morning, going over it all again—it was a subject he seldom talked about--I regret once more what I didn't do and didn't say at the time. Surely it would have been easier for him if we'd talked more about how he felt. I don't like these moments of wanted to live it over, but they keep coming. Sometimes I feel as if I didn't deserve Len.

Meals seem to be a dangerous time for him. Tonight at dinner, he's already at the table and in a foul humor when I get there. He demands to know why no one's paying attention to him because he needs food. When I get something for him, he pushes it away; he isn't going to eat this shit, no way. I remove the plate and bring him some custard, which he usually professes to like. He isn't happy with me, and keeps muttering in a low voice that I lack a sense of humor—which is certainly true at that moment. I get him out of the dining room as quickly as possible and we begin the nightly routine. When I leave, he tells me once again that I'm his backstop and he's afraid I'm not going to stick around much longer.

***

Len has an appointment with our eye doctor this morning. I should have arranged for the wheelchair van to take us, but that's a bore and I think we can manage on our own. This is a mistake, as every aspect of the expedition proves challenging. First, I have trouble getting the walker into the backseat of the car and have to jam it into the trunk. Then the most convenient handicap spaces at the doctors' office are full and it's a long walk in the heat to get into the building.

Len complains every step of the way and I am tempted to abandon the whole idea. After all this, the diagnosis is a minor irritation in the eye—no treatment recommended. On the way back here, Len announces he's falling apart, he doesn't have it together and he's drifting. I snap back that he shouldn't worry because that makes two of us, and then feel guilty. When we finally get back to his room, both of us exhausted and cranky, he points to the engraving of the ship hanging over the TV. It is, he says, an example of our good life. He then turns to the photos on the bureau and tells me who they are. Along with the ship, they're his touchstones, his signposts in the unfamiliar landscape of his life.

His conversation is all over the place now. One of his frequent complaints is that I'm 100% and he's not, which, he always adds, isn't right. I wonder if he means he should be taking care of me, and not vice versa, which would be characteristic. As a matter of fact, I've always assumed he would always be there. He dwells on our financial situation obsessively, assuring me we're fine. I wonder if he's worried and is reassuring himself. Then out of the blue, he'll announce he doesn't give a shit about alcohol.

I spent last night in Little Compton with a friend. Sometime after midnight I start to get up to go to the bathroom, slip off the edge of the bed and land with a thud on the floor. I lie there for some time before struggling up and checking on the damage. Nothing seems broken, but I have a nosebleed and bruises and feel nauseous. I lie awake for the rest of the night with a pounding headache, fretting about the blood spots on my hostess's pristine pink rug.

I come back here right after breakfast, still haunted by the sound of my head hitting the floor. The weather is humid and thundery, which doesn't add to my good humor. The nurse diagnoses a mild concussion, for which the remedy is time and rest. Len is in one of his spacier moods. He says he's having trouble figuring all "this" out and it's all I can do to get him into bed at the end of the day before I collapse. Before leaving, I lie down with him for a while, which soothes us both. His physical presence comforts me because it hasn't changed--he even smells the same. I hope it helps him to be touched. People say it does, but does anyone really know?

The accident scares me. I know Paris would take over in a minute if I weren't here. She's at Bridges almost as much as I am and Len is as comfortable with her as with me. If anything, she's better with him than I am. But I would feel as if I was abandoning him and he might not understand why I wasn't there.

***

Paris, her daughter Sylvia and I have just returned from a few days with a cousin and her husband in Maine. I looked forward to the visit for weeks, although it was hard to decide to leave Len. We drove to Camden and went right out to the island, which is about an hour off shore. It was my first visit there without Len and it felt odd, as if something essential was missing, as indeed it was. The weather was ideal, with blue skies, calm seas and low humidity. It was perfect, except for missing Len. Sometimes it seems to me as if he's already dead, and for much of the world he is. To me, on the other hand, he's more alive than ever because he consumes my energies, my emotions and my thoughts.

I was amused by the relatively new dynamic of our threesome, grandmother, daughter, and granddaughter. Paris is in charge now and I'm the tagalong. When Paris was the little girl, I was in charge and my mother was the tagalong. It makes me smile to think that my mother must have felt the same as I do now, when she realized she wasn't the central figure anymore. In a way it's a relief to sit back and be told what to do.

One morning we took a long hike around the island. I managed to keep up with the others, but it wore me out and I was nervous about tripping and falling after the recent bed episode. The last time Len and I were on the island, he was recovering from prostate surgery. We were sleeping in the so-called guesthouse, a converted bait house on top of a steep slope behind the main house. When he got up at night, he urinated off the porch while I listened, envious of how easy it was for a man. Now there's a guestroom in the house and a chemical toilet. I slept like a log, but I woke up each morning feeling guilty I was having a pleasant time, while Len might be lying awake wondering where I was.

The joke's on me, because according to Ames, who was left in charge, Len didn't seem to know I was gone. He asked once in a while where I was, but it was enough to tell him I'd be back soon. He didn't seem surprised to see me when I reappeared. In fact, the first thing he said to me was that I must be crazy. I can't remember the context, but maybe it was a form of transference. Ames reported that while I was away, Len got in another altercation with the volunteer who comes in to lecture the residents about current affairs. I wish the aides would keep them apart. Both parties are guilty, but I refuse to find Len responsible.

***

Len complains all the time that he's getting screwier. He talks about going home and how nice it'll be when we can eat together again. He says he's being jerked around and nothing I can say soothes him. Tonight he announces loudly at the supper table that I, meaning me, don't have any gray hair. I suggest he look a little closer. He laughs and says that unlike him, at least I have hair.

We've had more battles over shaving lately and I don't know why I don't just leave it alone. Because he gets so breathless when he walks, most days we just sit in the courtyard. There's a new resident in Bridges who's often out there with her husband. She's a diminutive woman, almost doll-like. At meals the husband feeds her, one mouthful at a time. One day he brought in a dish of melon cut up with toothpicks, so she could manage it by herself. With great effort she picked up the pieces up one by one and ate them.

This morning I go to Little Compton for a memorial service for a friend who died earlier this summer. It's held on the lawn of their house, with a view out over the fields and down to the reservoir below. I always wonder if Len will be next. When I get back, he's in a bad mood and keeps saying he doesn't want to pick a fight with me. The mood passes when Ames arrives and I'm reminded of how Len and I would stop quarreling when one of the children appeared so as not to upset them. His dark moods sometimes take an odd form. One night in the dining room when he'd been loudly angry, he announced that at least he hadn't been kicked out of the club yet.

The seizures continue. One afternoon, I find him on the bed, speechless, with his right hand up in the air, and he doesn't recover for over an hour. I've never gotten used to these episodes. There's been a problem with the laundry lately. The residents' clothes and sheets and towels are all washed together and then tossed into big hampers. The aides are supposed to sort it out, but they seldom have the time and many of the clothes aren't marked. I've fallen back on retrieving Len's things as soon as possible, but whatever I do, things go missing. I bought two sets of sheets when Len moved in, along with myriad pairs of t-shirts, socks and pajamas. When they disappear, I replace them at Wal-Mart.

His pants come from an Internet site that sells clothing for nursing home use, all of it ugly, with openings in the most amazing places. Len was never a clotheshorse, but he wouldn't be happy if he knew about the Wal-Mart underwear.

Our anniversary was early in the month, on the 10th. When I mentioned it to Len, he connected for a moment and then forgot. When I brought it up again later, he said he didn't remember much about the wedding, but he knew we'd had a good life. Our wedding seems like yesterday, and at the same time a million years ago. Whatever we may have thought we knew then, the wedding vows were just words. They've acquired meaning only as experience has charged them with significance. So many anniversaries have come and gone, some better than others, but each one marking another year together. Sometimes we did nothing, sometimes we had a party, and other times we took a trip.

XXII

One of Those Trips: The Views From the Top

We took a trip to celebrate our 45th wedding anniversary. Eager to stay in one place, we rented a house in Roussillon, a hill village in Provence, in southern France. We'd seen the village a few years earlier and admired its situation on top of looming red-yellow cliffs. Friends knew someone who had an available house there, and we decided to give it a try. It was September when we arrived, so the summer crowds had gone home. We were immediately struck by the beautiful views radiating out in all directions from the town, but we soon learned that enjoying them required a lot of climbing, both up and down.

Even getting around our house, which was called *La Petite Maison Rouge*, was challenging. Like many others in the village, it was built on multiple levels. Thus the living room and kitchen were on the ground level, with the bathroom and the bedrooms below it. There was a terrace off the living room, where we spent most of our time when we were not out. Partially roofed over, it housed a collection of old pots and garden tools, a clothesline and a rickety table and chairs. It's main feature, however, was a gorgeous view of the landscape.

Every morning during those two weeks, we set out early to buy the *International Herald Tribune* and something for breakfast. The walk began easily enough, with a stroll across the square in front of the house. We continued on down a sloping street to the market square and the newsstand. The bakery was next, and it always took a long time to decide which delicious item to take home. Should it be a croissant or a brioche or a lovely loaf of bread? Our return trip took us up the steep stone staircase that led back to the higher part of the village. It wasn't easy going, especially for my short legs. Len, who is long-legged, sprinted ahead of me, occasionally glancing back to offer a word of encouragement. Once we made it to the top, however, the view of the countryside was reward enough.

There were other attractions too, like the elegant red house built into the cliff, which was surrounded by an array of potted plants. Cats were just coming out to sun themselves in their doorways and a few dogs were enjoying their first walk of the day. If the tiny beauty salon had opened, we'd see an early customer or two sitting under the ancient dryer. By the time we got back to our square, the café owners were busy setting out tables and hosing the sidewalks off in preparation for the tour buses that would soon labor up the hill to disgorge their passengers for the day.

Everywhere we went in the surrounding countryside, there were more beautiful views. One hot morning, we climbed up to the highest point of *Les Baux*, a medieval fortress built on a site once inhabited by primitive man. The panorama from its crumbling ramparts illustrated the convenience of living on a hilltop in the absence of modern forms of communication; what

167

was merely a view for us might have meant survival for the inhabitants.

But some of the less dramatic prospects were amazing. One afternoon we hiked up a steep path that began in a village called *Oppède-le-Vieux, Oppède-le-Jeune* having grown up at a less taxing altitude below. Our objective was a ruined eleventh-century-church I'd read about in the guidebook. Perhaps its founders had built on a hill because it felt safe, but their less hardy successors had abandoned the old church for a more accessible site. It was almost four o'clock by the time we reached our goal, an hour when the famed Provencal light is at its most evocative. Some prefer the misty glow of early morning, but the hint of melancholy of the hours between 5 and 7 PM has its own special charm. That afternoon, the September sun fell aslant, descending with maternal softness on the fields of lavender covering the floor of the valley below us. Bathed in the honey-colored light, the rows of trimmed plants stretched as far as we could see.

Only an occasional flash reflecting off the cars on the road in the middle distance interrupted the timelessness of the scene before us. The sun shone benevolently, turning the worn stones of the little church to gold. A couple with a toddler joined us briefly, but the child strayed too near the edge of the precipice for comfort and they left, their little terrier trotting along behind as they disappeared down the narrow path. Once again we were alone in contented silence, that happy state of non-verbal communication that's the reward of a long relationship.

At the end of our two weeks, another beautiful view seemed to embody this same sense of silent communion. On the way to Nice to fly home, we stopped for a few nights in *St. Paul-de-Vence*. One of those nights we had dinner at a restaurant called *Le Coleur Pourpre*, a name that puzzled me. Why would a French restaurateur choose the name of an American novel? But when we got to the restaurant and saw the cascades of magenta Bougainvillea tumbling around the doorway, I had my answer, and Alice Walker had nothing to do with it.

The restaurant was built into the stone ramparts of the village and from our outside table we could see the curved stretch of the Cote d'Azur far below. We watched the lights of Nice and the towns beyond it twinkle on. At first a dim mound in the distance, the island of Corsica faded gradually from view. It was a gorgeous view, and a familiar one. In 1958 we were on a ship that was sailing from New York to Genoa. We stopped in Nice for an afternoon, rented a car and drove up the coast to Monaco--the very coast we were looking at. When the ship sailed out of Nice that evening, Corsica was visible off the starboard side. Standing in the stern of the ship, we watched the dolphins playing in the wake until the sun set in the West. For a while that evening, the coast of North Africa was a shadowy shape to leeward.

Now, roughly 45 years later, we were looking down at that same sea, and we'd changed as much as the landscape. Our youth was gone, but in our time together we'd gained the deep sense of companionship we'd shared on the steps of the church a few days before, and shared now. Gazing out over the Mediterranean, we ate a wonderful meal and drank a bottle of pale pink wine. Being young had been wonderful, but this was better.

XXIII

A Fall

The last weeks of Len's life begin with a phone call early one morning in late August. It's an aide, telling me he's fallen. When I get to his room, he's lying sprawled on the floor near the bathroom, his left leg bent at an odd angle and one elbow bruised and bloody. He looks like a broken doll. When the ambulance has taken him away, I go back to the apartment and get dressed, drive to the hospital and find him in the ER.

When he's wheeled off for x-rays I go to the cafeteria and try to eat breakfast, but the oatmeal tastes like sawdust and I can't finish it. When I return to the ER, Paris has arrived and we wait while Len is taken in and out. After a few hours, Paris sends me home. I've been sick and and she doesn't think it's safe for me to be in a hospital. On the way out, I run into a surgeon friend. When I tell him what's happened, he shakes his head and says something like this is inevitable, a predictable part of the downward spiral for someone as fragile as Len.

Ames joins Paris and they stay with Len all day, phoning me frequently to report. The x-rays show a fractured left hip, but the two of them, along with the doctors, make the decision not to operate. The consensus is that with his heart condition and lack of mobility, Len's recovery would be difficult, let alone the operation.

I lie on the bed all day, conflicted, sorry not to be at the hospital but relieved that someone else is making the difficult decision, which I know is the right one. Health directives, living wills, etc. are all very well, but when the time comes to make a life or death decision, there are no easy answers. Around four in the afternoon, Len is brought back to a room on the nursing floor at Epoch. He's groggy from painkillers, confused and agitated--he looks so sad, just a weary, unshaven old man. I feed him a little supper, but all he wants is to sleep and I soon leave and come back here and try to adjust to our new world.

From that moment on, I feel suspended in time, living in the moment, and sure of nothing except that everything has changed. I know—we all know--the hip isn't going to heal by itself. I can't think of a better way to convey a sense of what those weeks were like than to quote from my journal, as I have all along, but this time without any interruptions. Those few weeks were a bad time for our children and for me, but most of all for Len. Given the reality of the fall, I don't think his final days could have been different, but that doesn't stop me from wishing they hadn't been so hard because he deserved better.

***

It's Labor Day weekend, and a year since we moved here, which is very hard to believe. Len seems a little brighter today, but he's very foggy. He keeps repeating, "I can't, I can't" over and over again. He's done it before, but now he sounds desperate. He blurts out that he can't seem to keep score, and then five minutes later says he's fine. I can't imagine what the suddenness of the fall, the day in the ER, and now the strange room, have been like for him, piling confusion upon confusion.

The food on the nursing floor is terrible—his lunch today is a gray hamburger on a dry bun with a glob of gluey potato salad. Len manages a few bites, but he lacks the energy to chew. He enjoys the pudding and attacks it awkwardly with a spoon in his weak left hand. His aides say he's in a lot of pain and they're giving him more Percocet, which makes him fuzzier.

The social worker on the floor asks my permission to transfer Len to a semi-private room. The only one available is the smallest double on the floor, with two of everything jammed into it. She tells me he'll be moved after lunch so he can settle in before bedtime, which seems sensible. I arrange for Paris and me to meet her in the new room to discuss Len's care, but when we arrive at the appointed hour, a man who looks near death is in the bed designated for Len—and there's no sign of the social worker. We retreat to the old room, where the nurses tell us there's been a delay. Len is finally transferred at 5:30—heaven knows what happened to the other man. By then Len is exhausted. The second bed in the room is empty and we hope it stays that way.

***

After a blissfully quiet week, the second bed in Len's room is occupied by a man who has the TV on all day, even when he's asleep. If the curtain is pulled between the two sections, there's not enough room for anything but the bed and the bedside cabinet. Every morning, the aides put Len in a wheelchair, where he sits slumped over and staring into space. He asks continually to go back to bed, but the aides don't like to move him because it's difficult for them and painful for him. Mostly he drowses or stares intently at the photographs on the bedside table. He seems to be looking for something on the wall, and I wonder if it's the engraving of the ship that's in his room in Bridges.

He keeps saying I should put him away and the life seems to have gone out of him. He's supposed to go to the dining room for meals, but it's difficult to get the wheelchair close enough to the table and the tremor in his hands makes it hard for him to hold a spoon or a fork. He spills a lot, and then gets discouraged. When Paris or I try to feed him, he quickly tires of it and pushes the food away.

This morning I go with him to a physical therapy session, in the basement of Epoch. I ask the therapist what they can possibly do for him and he tells me they're trying to build up the strength in his arms and his good leg. Len does his best to follow directions, but he can't focus. It looks to me like an exercise (maybe exercises?) in futility.

This afternoon Paris and I meet with the social worker and the head nurse. They tell us if we stop Len's physical therapy, his Medicare coverage ends. The rules dictate that to retain coverage, a "plan of recovery" must be submitted every three weeks. This makes no sense, as whatever else happens, Len is not going to "recover." They don't have an answer when I ask how they plan to define his recovery, so, no more therapy. During Len's earlier medical dramas, we always had hope. The direction of the narrative was positive, with an outcome we could look forward to even if it was a compromise. I've known for at least a year this story would end badly, but as long as the end was invisible I could ignore it—no more.

***

This was a difficult day. To begin with, it's Sunday, when the nursing help is scarce and/or inept. In the morning I find Len lying naked on a heap of urine-soaked bedding. When this happened in Bridges it was bad enough, but now he's completely helpless. His glasses are nowhere in sight and searching for them under the bed, I find a stray pill that missed its target. I round up two aides from another room, who finally wash Len and get him into the wheelchair. Then I notice that the abrasion on his elbow hasn't been dressed. Finally the RN on call takes care of it, and even locates his glasses, which were next to the TV in the lounge.

***

I was awake most of last night pondering Len's situation. This morning I tell the social worker we want Hospice to evaluate him. She tries to talk me out of it, and keeps asking if we understand the "implications "of the decision. I assure her we do. He's in constant pain, his condition is worsening and we want him made comfortable and left alone to rest in peace. Next I go to Bridges and give up the hold on his room, which I should have done sooner. I can't imagine I ever thought Len would go back there, but it seemed like abandoning hope to assume otherwise. The curtains were closed and the room looked so empty. We lived in that room for a year. I never thought I'd miss it, but it holds the last moments of our life together.

***

Len has been in Epoch for nearly three weeks now and September is more than half over. "Nurse Pat" from Hospice comes to evaluate him this morning. She reviews his extensive medical history with me and seems astounded he's alive. I find her kind and intelligent, and to my relief she accepts Len as a Hospice patient, so even before the day ends, there's progress. A bulky lounge chair on wheels is delivered right after lunch. It takes up most of the floor space in his room, but looks more comfortable than the wheelchair. The aides have to use a lift to move Len from the bed to the chair. It's a complex piece of equipment that hoists him up in a canvas and net square. He's a vision, his long legs and arms dangling over the edges of this, and he protests loudly in his most colorful language.

Len seems happy enough once he's in the chair, which is on wheels. Unfortunately, it's even harder than the wheelchair to manage in the dining room. At supper tonight, I keep hitting his leg on the edge of the table, which is painful for him. I always try to encourage him to feed himself, but he soon gets impatient. Tonight he says repeatedly he doesn't "advocate this." Phrases get stuck in his brain and then repeated over and over again.

***

Now that he's used to the lounge chair, Len seems happy to spend his day in it. The aides park him by the TV in the lounge and he sits there snoozing along with the other residents. He soon slumps down, but still seems more comfortable than the wheelchair. I'm reminded of Mr. Smallweed in Dickens's *Bleak House*, a disagreeable old man who keeps slipping down in his chair and having to be "shaken up" by his cantankerous niece.

This afternoon I talk with both the Hospice nurse assigned to Len and their chaplain. The offer of help from the latter was so heartfelt that I hesitate to admit to her I'm not a good candidate for a support group. I fudge, which is silly, but it's such a relief to be offered help that I don't want to sound ungrateful. There's an article in today's paper explaining the term "GOMERS," an acronym used by ER personnel to refer to debilitated and/or demented old people: it's short for "Get Out of My Emergency Room." We've been the victims of that attitude, and Hospice's kind treatment is a revelation.

Len's sister Katharine comes to see him this morning, along with one of his female cousins. He seems to recognize his sister, and then lapses back into a semi-doze. He smiles at the cousin, but I don't think he knows who she is. They both handle the situation well, but I find myself longing for him to respond. We all know it's the last time they'll see him alive, but no one mentions it.

***

Earlier this week I go to a party in Little Compton and spend the night with a friend. Sometime after midnight, I dream about 10 Meadow Lane as it was before we renovated it. When I fall asleep again, I dream about our house in Providence, except it's been relocated to the street in Northfield where I lived with my parents. I must have been in a mood to revisit the past.

In the morning, I take a long walk on the beach and breath in the sea air, rich with the scent of salt and honeysuckle and autumn clematis. When I get back here, Paris and Ames meet me in Len's room and we try to feed him some lunch. It's harder to hold his attention now. At one point he begins to chew the nylon straps on his lift, which is always under him. This can't be comfortable, but I suppose it blends in with his general discomfort. When I arrive, he stares at me intently and says it's time for him to go. At such moments he seems semi-aware of his situation. When Paris arrives, his face lights up as it always does when he sees her, and he greets her with a hearty "Hi, Sweetie.

I've just finished reading an interview with the writer Salman Rushdie in today's *Times*. I'm no great fan of his work, but I was struck by his reaction to the fatwa issued against him:

. . . one of the ways I expressed it to myself was that my picture of the world got broken. I believe we all have that—we all have a picture of the world we live in and we think we know what shape it has and where we are in it. Another word for it would be sanity. And then suddenly it was very difficult to know what shape the world was and where I stood in it and how to act.

Coincidentally, the interviewer was Charles McGrath, whom we met at a dinner party back when the

177

world was a known shape, to borrow a phrase from Rushdie. I can't imagine a universe without Len. I don't know where I belong and nothing makes any sense without him. I felt a similar sense of dislocation when my parents died, but then I had Len.

***

Nicholas comes for dinner and the night. We see Len early in the morning and wait while the aides clean him up, always a lengthy process. He greets Nicholas as if he knows who he is, but a few minutes later he asks me his name. Nicholas has to leave, but Paris and I are there this morning when the Hospice aide arrives to bathe Len. A large black man, he is amazingly gentle. We try to help him, but his skills surpass ours by a long shot--Paris is pretty good at it. She's been through this before, with her husband. It makes me sad to watch her.

The Hospice nurse comes in and we talk about moving Len to their nearby facility. However, she feels he's better off at Epoch because moving him would be so painful, which we accept. She orders his morphine increased and puts him on a soft diet. I'm going to insist on feeding him in his room because getting him to the dining room is painful and he's more apt to eat if he's comfortable. He hardly touches his lunch. I don't remember his precise words, but before I leave he says yet again it's time for him to go, in almost those words. I tell him I love him and he says he loves me too, adding, with a ghost of a smile, "Baby."

***

Every day brings a change for the worse. It takes a long time to bathe Len this morning because he's so weak and in such pain. As the day wears on, he peers intently at me, and whispers that he needs me. There are moments when we seem to communicate, but perhaps this is an illusion. He gets morphine pretty much on demand now.

In mid-afternoon I come back to the apartment briefly and return to find that Len is in the dining room, which enrages me. Wedged up against the table in the lounge chair, he's wincing in pain. I can't connect with him—it's as if he can't hear me. He tries to eat a mouthful or two, and then gives up. I think I hear him say he doesn't know how to turn himself off, yet again.

***

I have such a bad night that I call the Hospice chaplain--I should have known better. She assures me that Len's pain is of the moment while mine is constant, which isn't much consolation because it doesn't ease it for him. She suggests I find an hour or two a day to "put the burden down," but that's impossible. I can't concentration on anything and so I play endless games of solitaire on the computer.

Hospice's orders are that Len is not to be moved from bed any more. This morning he's moaning so loudly I ask for more pain medication. The nurse is reluctant to give it to him and he clenches the bedrails, his knuckles white and his face contorted. Occasionally he cries out. Since he's always had a high pain threshold, I don't like to think what he must be feeling. As I'm leaving, a Hospice volunteer comes in with a little white dog freshly groomed and with a big red bow around its neck, but Len barely responds to it—so unlike him, the animal lover.

He's been "upgraded" by Hospice, which means his pain medication will be increased. One of the nurses warns me this will make him less communicative, and that soon he'll stop eating and just sleep. They do everything they can to avoid the "die" word. Walking back here, it hits me I've just agreed to let him die, or at the very least I've hastened his death. It's the right thing, but I'd feel better if I could talk it over with Len.

***

Len is calmer and seems more comfortable now, but our relative peace ends when a man is moved into the empty bed in the room in the late afternoon today, along with a wife with a piercing voice. The poor fellow is confused, and they have a long conversation about his dentures. And would he like the urinal? Yes, he does, and the appropriate sound effects follow. The TV blares.

When I hear the wife say she'll there every day from 8 to 8, my heart sinks. As I'm leaving, she tells me she asked for a semi-private room on purpose because her husband likes company. I answer that since Len is dying, he won't be much good to him. This isn't nice, but I'm feeling desperate. I'm going to ask to have Len moved to a private room. We need a place where the children and I can be with him quietly.

***

Twenty-four hours later, Len dies. That morning, I see his condition has worsened, but I fail to register its seriousness—or perhaps I choose to ignore it. His faithful friend Hilary comes in at noon with pictures of a recent trip, but Len can't focus on them because he's had so much morphine. I leave to meet a friend for lunch. Len responds when I say good-bye and seems to know me. It's the last time I'll see him with his eyes open.

On my way out, I ask to have him moved to a private room. The nurse assures me it will happen the next morning, but when I get back a few hours later, he's already been moved. The change in him is dramatic. His eyes are closed, his breathing is slow and heavy and he's unresponsive. The new room is pleasant. There's a picture of the Sakonnet lighthouse on the wall opposite the bed, which seems fitting. A young Hospice nurse comes in to check on him and suggests I call Nicholas and tell him to come right away--yet still I fail to hear the message that the end is near. From then on, everything is surreal and I feel detached from what is happening.

Nicholas arrives in the early evening. Ames is there and Paris and we sit in the room listening to the rasping sound of Len's dying breaths, a sound I last heard some 24 years before, when my father was dying. Len's lips slowly turn blue. I can't stand just sitting there, so around 10 PM I go back to the apartment and get into my nightgown and lie down. About half an hour later, Nicholas appears in the shadow of the doorway to the bedroom and tells me Len died right after I left the room. I should have been with him until his last breath and I cannot imagine what I was thinking, if thinking is the right term for emotional paralysis.

His body is still warm when I get there, but as I hold him his hands grew cold and gradually, every part of him loses its warmth. Life departs so fast once it starts to go—I'd forgotten that. We sit with him for a few hours and the aides wash him and dress him in a clean gown. Two men from the funeral home came and take him away. We follow the gurney down the hall and then the children walk me back to the apartment; only then do I begin to realize what's happened.

The next morning we go back to Epoch for Len's belongings, which are waiting for us in two bulging garbage bags. Crammed in with the stained sheets and towels and the leftover shaving cream and toothpaste, are the t-shirts and socks from Wal-Mart and the pants with elastic waists and the sneakers with Velcro straps. On the bottom of the bag is a maroon baseball cap I bought him and an open package of Depends. It's all that remains of our year in Bridges.

That night I fall asleep early, only to wake up with a start at the same time Len died the previous night, which can't have been a coincidence. People have tried to make me feel better about leaving him. They've told me that often someone dies just as their loved one goes out of the room, to spare them. I would like to believe this was so—it would be typical of Len—but I don't.

XXIV

Saying Good-Bye

We're standing in a circle around Len's body, which lies in a cardboard coffin. There are no gold and white draperies this time, and instead of the Indian dress that Vishram wore at his cremation not so long ago, Len has on a pair of khaki pants and a blue and white striped LL Bean travel shirt, its collar frayed from wear. I wanted him to look comfortable.

We scatter flowers on his body and speak to and about him. I give him his passport, his glasses and a faded black-and-white photo of the two of us that was taken at a party the year before we were married. This morning's ceremony echoes Vishram's. When my parents died—and Len's parents and Paris's husband Henry—the bodies simply disappeared, but Len is here with us. After saying our good-byes, we follow him into the crematorium and watch as his body enters the fire. It feels to me as if he and Vishram are united in death. Then we walk around the cemetery for a little while. It's a chilly, grey day, with a low mist hovering over the river. I remember how he liked to see the swans.

On a wet Saturday a few weeks later, we bury Len's ashes in our family plot in the Union Cemetery in Little Compton. Originally laid out on land adjacent to the church, the cemetery has since spread across the road in an easterly direction. Our plot is in a section beyond the one filled with villagers who died in the nineteenth century. An even newer area has been cleared further to the east, but it too is filling up and soon there will be no more room. A path runs through the older graves to our plot, but this morning we drive in on the dirt road that runs behind the parish playground. Sheltered from the harsh winter winds, our graves are next to a hedge of the green privet that flourishes in the sea air. When we get out of the car, the custodian, who arrived earlier to cut a square in the ground, hovers discreetly behind the hedge, ready to replace the turf when we're done.

I picked up his ashes a week or so after Len's death. The box seemed larger than what the children had described to me after selecting it. Indeed, it was so heavy I had trouble carrying it to the car. When I got back to Laurelmead, the maintenance director met me and hurried me to the front hall. One of the men from the funeral home was standing with a stricken expression on his face, holding another box. It seemed he'd given me the wrong ashes. Looking at the box as it goes into the ground, I almost laugh to think of the potential mix-up, which would have amused Len.

We've been through this ritual several times before. In 1975, Len's father died suddenly at age 75, and was buried here on a mild autumn day. He was the first occupant of the plot that he and my father had purchased together. My mother came next, on a warm day in June when the peonies were in bloom. They were one of her favorite flowers and so we scattered petals from our bushes over her ashes. We buried my father on a cold February morning and my mother-in-law on an even colder New Year's Eve, when the custodian had to cut through the snow to dig the hole. Paris's husband Henry was next, and lastly, my mother's sister and her son, just before Len went into Bridges.

Now, so soon, it's his turn. It rained during the night and it's still sprinkling lightly and wet leaves flutter soundlessly down from the trees. Just as the service begins, our oldest grandson Gideon notices that I'm standing alone. He comes over and puts an arm around me, a gesture that threatens to bring on the tears I'm determined not to shed. When we buried Gideon's father, he was 8 years old. It had rained then too and the ground was still damp. His sister Sylvia, just 3, tripped over the hole prepared for her father's ashes and dirtied her beautiful yellow dress.

The minister says a few words and we sprinkle dirt on the box and then it's over. We walk back through the cemetery and into the church to wait for the memorial service to begin. The moment comes, and as Ames and I stand in the doorway waiting for our cue to walk down the aisle, I distance myself. If I pretend I'm not here, maybe Len won't be dead. Maintaining a measure of detachment becomes harder as the service progresses, but I manage and eventually it ends.

There's a reception afterwards at a local club. Len and I never liked these large gatherings, everyone talking loudly and trying to get to the buffet table so they can eat and leave. If he were alive and this was someone else's reception, we'd be debating how long we had to stay. At least Len is spared this one.

The last guest finally straggles out and we divide up the leftover food and leave. I drive back to Providence with Ames and Pascale and Juliette. It's dark and when we get there, the lights of the city glitter in the rain. Everything still seems at a distance. What I see most clearly is the box of ashes resting under the newly cut turf, in the dark. I think of the ending of one of Wordsworth's "Lucy poems," inspired by an early love of his who died young:

> No motion has she now, no force:
> She neither hears nor sees;
> Rolled round in earth's diurnal course,
> With rocks, and stones, and trees.

***

In the days and weeks and months that follow Len's death, I relive the last days of his life, over and over again. I remember how he looked slumped in his chair or trying to eat when he wasn't hungry or lying helpless in the sling that hoisted him into his chair towards the end. There's so much I still need to tell him, most of all that I wish I'd been a better wife. I'm sensitive to the self-indulgence of this line of thought. It's all very well to regret the past when there's no danger of reliving it, but I can't stop myself.

I read a lot about grief, not self-help books, but fiction and memoir. One of the few that makes any sense to me is Julian Barnes's *Levels of Loss*, about the death of his wife. There are many traps and danger "in grief," he writes, "and time does not diminish them. Self-pity, isolation, world-scorn, an egotistical exceptionalism; all aspects of vanity." He elaborates on the mourner's need for attention: "Look how much I suffer, how much others fail to understand: does this not prove how much I loved?"

And was loved, I might add, because it's hard to accept that the person who loved me the most is gone. I'm guilty of every one of the feelings Barnes cites, as well as plain garden-variety grief. In an essay about old age and death in a recent *New Yorker*, Roger Angell records a brief conversation with a therapist after his wife's death. He says to the therapist, "I don't know how I'm going to get through this." After a while the therapist answers, "[N]either do I, but you will." I too will "get through" this, or get better, because the only other options are chronic depression, suicide or physical collapse, none of which are attractive alternatives.

People ask me how I am and I say I'm fine—automatically, the way one does. I'm not fine and I'll never be fine again, not as when Len was alive. From now on, "fine" will be relative. I think of that scene in James's *Portrait of a Lady*, of Isabel Archer sitting in front of a dying fire and trying to imagine her future. More than ever, I see a blank wall cutting off the possibility of any sort of life without Len. I don't remember what it was like before there was him.

But I get better. It doesn't happen all at once and it's not consistent. The hours of black misery return again and again and I suspect they always will, but some days there are fewer. Many things, from the mundane to the minor, have the power to bring on, as abruptly as one of Len's seizures, an intense physical longing for him. It can be a certain food, a change in the seasons, the light on the ocean in Little Compton or a grandchild's fleeting resemblance to him. Yet I get up every morning and cope with the day and I haven't lost my mind to loneliness, at least not permanently. I think he would be proud of me, but if so, if I'm managing, it's thanks to him and the love he gave me.

XXV

At the Ranch

It's July 2013, less than a year after Len's death. Ames and I sit side by side on the rocks at the mouth of an Indian cave, part way up the side of the canyon that lies just to the north of the ranch house. We're so high up it looks tiny from here. The climb seemed harder than it used to, but with the help of the walking stick, I made it. We're looking southeast out over the undulating grasslands of eastern New Mexico. Only a few patches of green interrupt the sweep of brown because of the drought that's plaguing the Southwest. In the middle distance are the Turkey Mountains, a low wooded range stretching from north to south, home to herds of elk and wild turkeys. The first time Len and I saw a wild turkey was in those woods. We could hardly believe our eyes, but now they're everywhere.

The cave is one of the many Indian relics scattered around Fort Union Ranch's ninety-some thousand acres. This unique property is part of a trust set up at the end of the nineteenth century by a forbearer of Len's, General Benjamin Butler, a controversial figure in the annals of the Civil War.

He acquired the land after the war in what can only be termed a land grab, typical of the exploitation of the West in those years. He never saw the land, but he sent his son-in-law Adelbert Ames, also a general in the war, to survey the purchase. Some of the documents in the ranch's library suggest the local people still feel they were robbed.

For some years now, family members have been able to rent the ranch house during the summer months. Set in the midst of thousands of uninhabited acres, it's a haven of natural beauty and quiet. The nearest town is Las Vegas, New Mexico, forty minutes to the west and after the sun goes down, the stars are the only visible lights as far as the eye can see. I've come to spend a week here with our three children and most of our grandchildren. Many of them have been on the ranch before, working, visiting or both, but for others it's new. Every time Len and I came out here, we brought family or friends with us. He loved the ranch life, especially the riding, and sometimes joked about being reborn as a rancher. He would have been a good one.

Our last trip to the ranch was in September 2008, right after Obama's first nomination and during the early days of the Great Recession. Three couples, all good friends, were with us. It was a moment of simultaneous hope and fear, hope for the election of an inspirational young president and fear of an economic collapse. One day when the eight of us were in Las Vegas, we noticed that an old storefront on the town square was sporting an Obama banner. The sole staffer was an enthusiastic young woman, a medical student, taking a semester off to work for the campaign. There she was, essentially in the middle of nowhere, working for a man about whom she knew almost nothing. When Obama carried the state in November, I thought of her.

Len's health problems had begun by then, but he seemed well enough to risk being 45 minutes from the nearest hospital. Since the official summer season had ended and the ranch hands-- usually young family members—had left, there was no riding. I was fine with this, as the last thing Len needed was another knock on the head. A fearlessly enthusiastic rider, he'd taken more than one spill on previous visits. So instead of riding every morning, we hiked and explored the far reaches of the ranch in a truck. On the morning we left, I noticed Len out in the paddock talking to the horses, who'd come in from the range for their morning grain. He looked very much at home and I was sorry he'd missed the chance to ride one more time. I watched him, sensing that he wouldn't be back here, and that he knew it.

When we drove out to the main highway and back to the world later that morning, I wondered if I'd want to be at the ranch without Len, and when our children asked me to join them there the summer after his death, I hesitated. Would I miss him too much? Could I handle the noise and confusion of a large group? Would I be a burden? Then I thought of my mother-in-law. When she became a widow, her philosophy was to say yes to almost any proposal. Sometimes she got in trouble, but more often her willing spirit made life much more interesting. So I summoned up my courage and bought a plane ticket.

The trip got off to a bad start. My granddaughter Sylvia, Paris's husband Jim and I were slated to fly from Providence to Albuquerque via Chicago. We left at dawn, but were delayed in Chicago for eight long hours. Thus we arrived in Albuquerque—where Paris met us--in the evening instead of the afternoon, and reached Santa Fe even later. When I went to bed at midnight, my back aching and my head hurting from the change in altitude, I wondered what I'd gotten myself into.

Nor did I feel much better the next morning, but there was nothing to do but forge ahead. On our way to the ranch, we stopped in Las Vegas to shop for food and have lunch. The town looked the same as ever, depressed and almost empty. We bought as many supplies as would fit into our cars and then drove east until we got to Watrous, the tiny community that's the official address of the ranch. When we turned onto the long road leading into the ranch, I remembered how I'd felt when I'd last seen it, and my foreboding sense that Len would not be with me the next time.

If Las Vegas hadn't changed, neither had the ranch. The landscape we drove through on the way in looked the same, except the big waterhole a few miles in from the highway was a dust bowl. We passed Fort Union, the site of the remains of the fort, now a national monument. The ruts of the northern branch of the Santa Fe Trail run past it and continue on in front of the ranch and through the valley.

Fort Union was active right up through the Civil War and then gradually ceased to be important. The family gave the land on which it stands to the government some years ago, in return for a paved road almost all the way to the ranch. Across the road and up against the side of a mesa I could see the crumbling ruins of the old arsenal, and beside it the neglected graves of the soldiers and their wives and children who died far from home.

A few miles more, and we bumped over the bars of the cattle guard onto the dirt road that winds down past the cattle corral and to the ranch house. Invisible until the last minute, there it was, nestled into the side of a mesa and looking much as it had the first time we saw it. A simple, low stucco building with a tin roof, the house sits in front of a small pond bordered by willow trees that takes up most of the so-called lawn. The spring that feeds the pond makes a continuous low gurgle, the only sound one hears at night except for the hum of insects and the trill of an occasional bird.

As we drove around the back of the corral and over a second cattle guard into the driveway, it seemed to me that Len must be there. He might be sitting on the porch, cleaning the algae out of the pond or talking to the horses. I'd been back to many of our special places since his death, but few of them had provoked such an intense sense of his absence. I started to cry, but Nicholas hugged me and I felt a little better.

All that week, Len was with me. I don't believe in ghosts, but I do believe those we've loved live on as long as we who knew them are alive. There's hardly been an hour since their deaths when my parents were absent from my thoughts, and now Len. It's unacceptable to think I'll never see them again. When I dream about them, especially Len, waking up to reality is painful. In John Milton's *Sonnet XXIII*, the speaker dreams that his dead wife, her face veiled, leans forward to embrace him, but "I waked, she fled, and day brought back my night." The fact of Milton's blindness increases the poem's poignancy, but I suspect the feeling of darkness and loss is true for everyone who's lost a beloved.

The wrenching sadness of those first hours at the ranch passed, but I never stopped missing Len. When the feeling was most intense, I'd climb up the mesa in back of the house, find a snake-free rock and sit down and cry. But balancing the sadness were many happy moments, like our grandchildren's nervous delight as they rode out of the corral on the first morning, and our children's pleasure in being back at a place where they'd been young. I could sense the three of them reliving the past too, and perhaps trying to reconcile what they'd become with what they'd hoped to be.

It was a noisy and often chaotic household. Sometimes I got cross and impatient because I wasn't in charge anymore, although taking a metaphorical back seat is generally a relief. I got tired trying to do things that used to be easy because I wanted to be with everyone, even when it was too much. One morning I crawled up the side of a rocky canyon on horseback, hanging onto the mane for dear life and wondering if I'd lost my mind and what would happen if I fell. Another time I clambered into the back of the ranch's battered old truck and bumped over the rocky roads, my back aching every inch of the way. I did these things for myself, but also for Len because I needed to do them for him.

Sometimes at breakfast, when everyone was swirling around the kitchen, bumping into each other and arguing over who would get the last banana or the rest of the maple syrup, I felt life coming full circle. Len's and my story was ending, but our children's and grandchildren's would continue and we would live on through them. Our children are the age now Len and I were on our first visit to the ranch, when I couldn't have imagined the scene before me, a scene so rich in love and life.

Perhaps the most weighted moment of the visit came the morning I got up before dawn with my grandchildren to watch the sun rise over the valley. Our oldest grandson, who was working on the ranch for the summer, drove us to a high mesa not far from the ranch. We scrambled up the slope—the young went higher than me--and sat shivering in the chilly darkness to wait for daybreak.

Finally, a few rays of light appeared over the distant hills, mere slivers of gold at first. A few minutes more and we could see the valley begin to materialize before us. Slowly, very slowly, it filled with light, until the landscape was visible as far as we could see in every direction. I felt my spirit expand with the light and break through the familiar walls of grief that had enclosed it for so long. It only lasted a few minutes, but somehow I knew such moments would come again and yet again, and that in time I would see a way ahead.

Postscript

A day or two before Len's death in 2012, 10 Meadow Lane was sold for a second time. A few months later, a Little Compton friend called to suggest I take a look at what had happened to the house. So one day I drove down the lane, turned around in a neighbor's driveway and went back past the house; the view from that perspective had always been my favorite. But the house wasn't there. Instead, I found myself looking at a foundation with a few partial walls left standing at either end. The two decks were gone and in their place loomed mounds of dirt and stone. It looked like the photographs of Georgia after Sherman's march through the city during the Civil War.

I couldn't breathe. I felt as if I'd been hit hard in the stomach. I sat there in shock, my arms around the steering wheel and my head down, sobbing. It was as if our life in that house had been wiped out. No more could I pretend to see my family there, not even the shadows of our ghosts. My tears finally stopped and I drove out of Meadow Lane. Perhaps it was better this way and at least Len wasn't alive to see the death of the house he loved. I've never believed time can be reversed or stopped, and now there was nowhere to look but ahead.

41993241R00113

Made in the USA
Middletown, DE
28 March 2017